Dr. Nelson K. Williams

KINGDOM LEADERSHIP

A guide for sacred and secular leadership

Contents

Foreword 1

RICH WITH SOLID tenets of leadership and practical steps and reminders for leaders and aspiring leaders in all walks of life, Dr. Williams' experience, deep faith, and personal commitment to his own calling to lead elevates this practical primer from a "how to do" manual, to a "how to BE" philosophy. The reader is drawn into Williams' own experiences and learns how leadership lessons play out in real-world examples. Ultimately, all are bound by agape love. Love for the people he leads and love for the One who leads him is evidenced in every page.

Based on the definitive book on leadership, The Bible, Kingdom Leadership is time well-spent for aspiring leaders, current leaders, and those who may be experiencing a dry spell in the execution of their call to lead. Dr. Williams reminds us that the character of leaders is important. He compels us to accept the responsibility to continue to grow in wisdom and discernment and that the recognized call to lead is only the beginning. Who is leading me? Am I really following Him? Do my daily actions point to Christ? These are the questions that will stay with me.

Carol P. Michaelides—MBA, Certified Professional Coach
VP and Co-Founder, Pendaran, Inc.
Ann Arbor, MI

Foreword 2

KINGDOM LEADERSHIP IS a book that should be read by all leaders, regardless of the industry that they are in. Whether the industry is government, academia, business, or even the church, all leaders should familiarize themselves with the golden principles within this book. Although these gems have been compiled in this great book for you to read, I had the honor of witnessing the principles in action by Dr. Williams before they were compiled into this valuable book.

Many years ago, I had the honor of first meeting Dr. Williams when we were both stationed with our families at Camp Walker and Camp Carroll, South Korea. I observed him discuss many of the principles within this book each day both in the church and in the military community. As a young Major, I was a Battalion Executive Officer and Operations Officer. I had the chance to work with him one-on-one in the maintenance shop that he oversaw as a Division Chief. During that time, my colleagues and I learned how to treat people the right way, cultivate a unified culture, and build great teams in the short two-year time frame when we were there. Without a doubt Pastor, Dr., and now Apostle Nelson K. Williams, taught me the principles that I needed to know to succeed as a General Officer.

As you will read in the book, I was called to be the Army's 66th Inspector General. I was required to have multiple years of assignments, locations, and experiences to prepare me for that position. As the Army's Inspector General, I worked for the Secretary and Chief of Staff for the Army, helping to solve many of the toughest problems in the United States Army. Without a doubt, I wish that I had the book *Kingdom Leadership* to give out to leaders from the general officer ranks down to the youngest levels in our Army. Overall, this book is a valuable tool that will help you to understand your strengths and weaknesses as a leader and give you the practical steps to build an effective team.

My final word of advice to you: Read the book cover to cover, take notes, ask yourself the challenging questions, and be ready to ask questions when Dr. Williams visits your location.

Lieutenant General Leslie C. Smith, USA (Retired)
The 66th Inspector General of the United States Army

Introduction

IN THIS JOURNEY, over the years, I have been exposed to great leaders as I've grown as a leader. I truly believe that I was divinely handpicked at a young age to be a leader. I found myself being thrust into leadership roles wherever I was located, whether in a sacred setting or a secular setting. I've been fortunate in my career over time to be positioned to observe great leaders in both settings from Bishops in sacred organizations to Military Generals and Senior executives in the halls of the Pentagon and various settings in successful organizations. Learning principles from these great leaders, as well as developing strategies of my own, have proven to be successful, which I will share with you in the chapters of this book. Throughout the years, I have been asked many times by men and women, young and old, for advice, counsel, strategies, and wisdom on effective leadership. These requests ranged from leadership as a pastor to leadership as an executive in the corporate arena. After many years of providing leadership principles and strategies, I was urged by many to share some of them along with my own experiences, observations, triumphs, and failures, which led to the creation of this book. This is not a comprehensive book on leadership, but I have provided some solid nuggets that will not only catapult your leadership to another level but promise to enhance your perspective on life.

GOD'S Kingdom Leadership

GOD'S KINGDOM IS His master plan. Your purpose and call to be a leader are tied to God's plan and are manifested to a greater degree. Because we have limited the word "calling" to professional ministerial occupation—that language distorts the divine nature and vastness of the creator of the universe. You have been called into His kingdom. Everything in the economy of God begins and ends with a call (1 PETER 2:9). When God calls us to do something, He calls us out of darkness into His marvelous light. The last call is the call to come home.

- COLOSSIANS 3:23 Whatever you do, work at it with all your heart, as working for the Lord, not for human masters, 24 since you know that you will receive an inheritance from the Lord as a reward. It is the Lord Christ you are serving.
- COLOSSIANS 3:17 And whatever you do, whether in word or deed, do it all in the name of the Lord Jesus, giving thanks to God the Father through him.
- COLOSSIANS 1:13 For he has rescued us from the dominion of darkness and brought us into the kingdom of the Son he loves.

Every Christian is part of the Kingdom. All work becomes Kingdom activity.

Kingdom Leadership is first the transformation of the person, second, the transformation of leadership, and third, social reform. As a Kingdom person, it is technically incorrect to make a difference between secular and sacred. If you are a Kingdom person, it all becomes Kingdom business. Whether you are washing dishes in a restaurant, the Chief Executive Officer (CEO) of a company, or a Pastor of a church, it is Kingdom Business. Secular is simply not spiritual; it is related to the physical world and not the spiritual world.

- **SECULAR** means outside of the church or religious setting.
- **SACRED** means inside the church or religious setting.

Some callings are performed in a secular setting, but you are called nonetheless. You can be called to be a businessman. Businessman in Hebrew means man of faith because business is a risk, and it takes faith to go into business. You must be called and anointed to do it. We are the Ecclesia, the Greek word for the "called-out ones." Jesus said go into all the world and teach the gospel. Therefore, we gather in the church buildings or assemblages for equipping and empowerment for that work. However, it's in the real world where the rubber meets the road. Don't neglect your leadership when you serve in church nor in the corporate world as some have. It works both ways. When you have the call of leadership on your life, no matter where you are, the divine call is on your life, nonetheless.

A career is what you are paid for, but a calling is what you are made for.

- If God calls you to do something, you were born for it.
- Some people think that only preachers have a divine call. This kind of thinking erroneously puts limits on a God who has no limits.
- Vocation is not just a particular activity or career; it is a function or station in life to which one is called by God.

What God calls you to is always greater than what He calls you from. Vocation is the state of being called. God calls us into our vocation. A vocation is a call from God to embrace a certain way of life and purpose. Our vocation allows us to use the gift God has given to serve Him and one another. Leadership and management are a calling and gift. You are not just educated to do it; you are divinely called to it. This is why it is unwise to choose a career solely based on the biggest salary. It must be a gift or a vocation. Every one of us comes into the world with specific God-given talents, gifts, and abilities. Don't bury it; use it (MATTHEW 25:14-30). This is why some experience internal turmoil in their career decisions. They struggle in those areas and experience stress because their current career is not their calling. One of the worst inward and obscure feelings is the feeling of being out of place. There is a special call to open a business, to work in government, to oversee, manage, and lead, etc. Some people discover that late in life. Nevertheless, once they find it, it comes naturally, and there is a great inward peace that brings a sigh of relief within. Once you discover your gift and calling, God will provide grace upon your life at every stage of your career.

Jesus said, "I will build my church (MATTHEW 16:18)" but He said to us, "Do business until I return (LUKE 19:13)." To do business is to make maximum use of your God-given gifts, talents, abilities, and opportunities. God is calling people to be strategically placed in several arenas, e.g. to be pastors, politicians, physicians, scientists, lawyers, CEOs, engineers, actors, actresses, singers, musicians, entertainers, entrepreneurs, and partners in leadership. You are essentially a kingdom man or woman but called to lead, sing, preach, write, teach, design, create, etc. You are graced to perform and fulfill the responsibilities in that particular profession or vocation. One's calling extends outside of the four walls of the church; it's a call to serve and be a change agent in the world.

In Genesis 41, Joseph was called and anointed by God to serve in civil government. He was used as an instrument of God, although he never preached a sermon in a church. He operated in secular government all the days of his life and was second in command to Pharaoh, and God put him there to serve His people.

Nehemiah was also called to work in government affairs. The entire book of Nehemiah provides modern-day leaders with a wonderful strategic model of leadership. Upon learning of the distress of his people, Nehemiah received permission from the king whom he was serving to go and help them. Despite obstacles and opposition, he discerned a challenging vision and led the people in accomplishing it. He was never one behind a pulpit but was divinely called to lead. While Nehemiah was the leader who first articulated the vision, the people confirmed the vision and committed themselves to the task. The gifts of all were required to achieve the vision. This is comparable to leading an executive staff in a military brigade today. Accomplishing the vision was not easy. Once people buy into you, they will more easily buy into your vision. Outside opposition made faithfulness very difficult. Yet, Nehemiah and the people persevered. He demonstrated true leadership and gained the trust of the people. This permitted Nehemiah to build a team that could make the vision happen. People shared the responsibility to accomplish the goal. No one person can accomplish a vision alone. Nehemiah began with a few, then he expanded the team to include virtually everyone, a key to successful leadership. The people committed themselves to the "common good" (NEHEMIAH 2:18). The talents, skills, and gifts of the people were identified, named, and utilized to build the organization (NEHEMIAH 3). Different people worked on different sections of the wall or projects comparable to their knowledge, skills, and abilities. People were assigned to work in the area of the wall that was closest to their homes. This was a leadership quality of putting people first. As they rebuilt the wall, they were ridiculed and mocked. Their enemies and competitors did everything possible to discourage them. They threatened to tell untrue stories about Nehemiah to discredit his name and brand. Nehemiah listened but persisted with wisdom and resilience. One of the keys to discernment and maturity as a leader is knowing what to ignore. Nehemiah knew that he was "doing a great work" (NEHEMIAH 6:3) and could not come down from the wall to debate with the enemies who only wanted him out of business. As a leader, you have to know the "Why." In other words, it is imperative that one knows why or understands the purpose of the mission and the importance of reaching the goal. This is why Nehemiah persisted even when adversity came. As I often say, you must keep the ball moving. True leaders don't give up when adversity comes. You have to create a structure or system for where you want to go. Where you sit determines what you see and how you think. God took Moses to a high place on the mountain and to a place in the Spirit to give him a greater perspective, God's perspective. A person in charge of an entire organization will see things differently than someone in charge of a department or unit in the organization. Don't be intimidated when you see someone on a higher level than you are, be motivated by it. Beware of comparing and competing with a dishonest objective. We are always on a journey with God. We rest for a brief time, but we do not stop. We keep seeking the new level that God is calling us to reach. God always has something else for us to do, a higher level and deeper depth that he wants to take us to. We cannot become what God wants us to be by remaining stagnant.

- A kingdom leader recognizes the supreme authority of God and is submitted to that authority.
- A kingdom leader understands the call to lead, regardless of the environment whether sacred or secular.
- A kingdom leader is explicit and intentional in expanding the Kingdom by focusing on the areas that maximize returns that enhance the Kingdom in terms of resources, land, influence, and power.
- A kingdom leader recognizes the human limits and develops the team by entrusting and empowering them to take responsibility and ownership in the Kingdom that they are growing together.
- A true kingdom leader has advisers and mentors but understands that God ultimately places, promotes, and grants positions of authority; thus, a kingdom leader makes all decisions in a manner that pleases God.

" *For the Kingdom of God is not a matter of talk but of power.*
1 CORINTHIANS 4:20

Leadership and Management in The Beginning

IN THE BEGINNING, God put Adam and Eve in management positions. He made man and gave him something to do—He gave him purpose.

> " *So God created man in his own image, in the image of God created he him; male and female created he them. And God blessed them, and God said unto them, Be fruitful, and multiply, and replenish the earth, and subdue it: and have dominion over the fish of the sea, and over the fowl of the air, and over every living thing that moveth upon the earth.*
>
> GENESIS 1:27–28

DOMINION is the power to rule; control of a country, region, etc. There are management principles that we can glean from the first human managers that God exposed us to in the Bible. Here they are:

1. **Take Responsibility.** (GENESIS 2:15, 3:12) Take responsibility for everything that happens under your watch. Know what is going on in your organization, unit, department, branch, business, etc. Ask for and read reports from your

executive staff and team members. This is not to say that you should be a micromanager. This is called positive intrusive leadership. It informs your team that you are interested in what they are doing and how they are doing. You do this by getting from behind the desk, visiting work areas, and by walking around, greeting and meeting individuals in the organization.

2. **Give your employees room to work and create.** We see that God gave Adam a large garden. The sheer amount of vegetation described hints at the amount of space. In the same way, our employees need space. If we are always looking over their shoulder into their workspace, we create an atmosphere that communicates we do not trust them. If we have hired the right people for the job, they should be able to achieve the principles, roles, and responsibilities that we give them, while having the space to work in a way that suits them best.

3. **Show interest and care for employee needs.** Not giving them enough space is unhealthy but making them feel abandoned and alone will often create the same result: an underperforming and unmotivated employee. We see God being active and aware in the Garden. He demonstrated positive intrusive leadership. Adam didn't have to figure out that he needed Eve, someone to help him manage; God was present enough to recognize and act on it. With our employees, we need to be consistent in engaging them in ways that motivate and inspire them. This will look different for each employee; as leaders, we should cater ourselves to them. If you don't value people, you can't add value to them. Some will request a one-on-one each week where they can run down their checklist of questions; others will desire a working lunch to ask questions and hear feedback, yet others will feel encouraged by you making time

to ask them about their family and sharing some things about your family in turn.

4. **Know Your Team Members.** (GENESIS 2:20) Know the names of your team members. Identify their strengths and gifts, and get to know and understand their personal and career goals, while offering career advice. Be their friend and show care and concern with wise boundaries. The Bible says those who have friends must also be friendly. Adam also showed emotional intelligence (EI) by taking time to meet and name all the animals in the Garden of Eden and not getting frustrated or angry at the volume or workload. We will talk more about EI in a later chapter.

5. **Have a mentor.** Mentorship is key if you want to succeed as a career executive and leader. You should subject yourself to someone whom you respect and look up to, especially in your chosen career path. It could also be a spiritual leader. You will learn more about this in the chapter on mentorship.

6. **Provide resources to your employees for success.** Adam had what he needed to work the garden because God made sure of it. When disparity did arise, he quickly moved to fix it; for instance, God created Eve. In the same way, we as leaders must be passionate about ensuring that we have given our people the resources necessary for success. Notably, Adam wasn't worried about his basic needs; he had food, water, shelter, etc. in adequate supply. As leaders, we need to support our executive staff, subordinates, and team in a manner that ensures they, too, have resources in adequate supply, which decreases stressors.

7. **Communicate the vision, mission, or purpose to your team members in a simple way, constantly.** Let them see how

being on the team or a part of the vision and mission will benefit their careers or benefit them personally (GENESIS 3:4–6). The Bible admonishes to write the vision and to make it plain, so those who read it can understand it and execute it (HABAKKUK 2:2). Keep the vision where they can see it, and repeat it to them as the opportunity presents itself.

8. **Always authenticate and verify information.** Confirm every report, by asking relevant and vital questions (GENESIS 3:6). Good communication is key to being an effective leader and to having a successful team. We will talk about the importance of asking the right questions in a follow-on chapter.

9. **Don't condone indiscipline and insubordination.** Openly but respectfully discipline members involved, to serve as a deterrent (GENESIS 3:8). Even when disciplining and counseling subordinates, you still have to respect them. Just because you are right, it doesn't give you the right to say it in a condescending manner. This speaks volumes moving forward and increases respect for you as a leader from the executive staff and subordinates.

10. **Give clear guidelines around your expectations.** As leaders, we have to own the process from communication to translation. Meaning, it is our responsibility to make sure the employee has internalized and personalized our expectations, not just heard them. It is imperative that not only you but your subordinates take ownership. Both Adam and Eve knew that they had sinned against God and violated policy because the expectations had been clearly communicated. They understood those expectations well enough to understand the seriousness of the consequences of working outside of the guidelines and/ or policy.

11. **Acknowledge their contribution and show compassion.** Adam was given a task to perform, and he performed the work of the task very well, although not perfectly. Even though Adam had a hand in bringing sin into our world, God still gave him credit for naming all the animals of creation. I believe we often forget that today. As leaders, we should prioritize thanking our employees and giving them accolades or recognition on the biggest stages possible, and be clear about what they have done to earn our praise and commendation. When there is failure, we should again recognize the result and not avoid the consequences, while at the same time showing compassion. Sometimes your greatest wisdom comes out of your greatest failure.

12. **Learn the Lessons.** God didn't shield Adam and Eve from the consequences of their actions, but he did provide them hope for a future in the midst of those consequences. Failure is not fatal, and failure is not final. As leaders, we do a disservice to those who follow us if we don't acknowledge their failure and show compassion appropriately to the incident. Truth and grace go hand in hand in management. The greatest lessons in life are not obtained in a course but on a course.

Divine Guidance

AS LEADERS, TODAY matters, this moment. We overestimate tomorrow, but we underestimate today. Previous leadership decisions are making us or breaking us. Daily, we are either repairing or fixing bad decisions from yesterday or preparing for tomorrow. There are about 400 leaders in the Bible but only a few of them maximized their days and finished well. As leaders, one of the secrets of success is determined by our daily agenda. Today, leaders put too much emphasis on decision-making versus decision-managing. We live in the information age where we have more access to knowledge than we have ever had in the history of the world, but yet we have the greatest deficit of wisdom. We have Siri, Google, Alexa, etc. However, there is a huge difference between knowledge and wisdom. To correct this, it takes Kingdom Leadership. More than ever, today, we need divine guidance. That's true Kingdom Leadership. Leadership decisions in this day and time are critical. The reality is that we live in a wicked world. The forces of evil make wrongdoing look attractive, especially in politics.

Lot was a leader who lost his family because he did not seek God's divine guidance for his career and family (GENESIS 18-19). Even as leaders and executives, we have to be careful not to sacrifice our families over our careers. When you follow divine guidance, you will know when the job or career move is right.

❝ *Trust in the Lord with all your heart, And lean not on your own understanding; In all your ways acknowledge Him, And He shall direct your paths.*
PROVERBS 3:5-6

❝ *Then spake Jesus again unto them, saying, I am the light of the world: he that followeth me shall not walk in darkness, but shall have the light of life.*
JOHN 8:12

In **NUMBERS 9:15-23,** the cloud and fire symbolized God's divine presence. God appeared to the children of Israel via a pillar of cloud by day and fire by night. It was by this that the people were led. It was a guide for both day and night. It was like a Global Positioning System (GPS). Moreover, the cloud kept the sun off of them during the day, which provided a cool shade, and the fire kept them warm at night. The cloud and fire were divine guidance and divine comfort.

When the cloud moved, they moved and when the cloud stopped, they stopped. As a leader, if you are not careful and discerning, you will be where God was, and not where He is. For example, you will be doing things the old, out-of-date way, rather than operating and moving with new strategies, technology, processes, programs, and policies. Many are using old methods but praying that God will do something new. Many leaders don't heed divine guidance but want guidance after they've made damaging corporate mistakes. Heed the divine signs, and learn from your mistakes, instead of repeating them.

You will experience divine moments in leadership. There will be divine meetings, and there will be divine interruptions. Every time Jesus was interrupted, a miracle ensued. God is known for doing divine work in the clouds, at high levels.

> **❝** *The LORD is slow to anger, and great in power, and will not at all acquit the wicked: the LORD hath his way in the whirlwind and in the storm, and the clouds are the dust of his feet.*
> NAHUM 1:3

> **❝** *Who layeth the beams of his chambers in the waters: who maketh the clouds his chariot: who walketh upon the wings of the wind:*
> PSALM 104:3

Many people whom you meet are not by coincidence. I have met people in the music industry who catapulted my music career; I have also met people in business who opened doors for me, and senior government officials who pushed me forward.

Don't Miss the Moment:
- Everybody you meet is either your student, teacher, or both.
- Surround yourself with people connected to your purpose.
- Get around people who are ahead of you.
- Get around those who challenge you.
- Get around those who push you out of your comfort zone.
- Get around those where growth is modeled and expected.
- Get around those who dream big for God.
- Get around those who are passionate.

5 Rules for Young Leaders
- You will learn lessons.
- There are no mistakes, only lessons.
- If you don't learn the easy lessons, they get harder.
- A lesson not learned will be repeated.
- You will know that you've learned the lesson when your actions change.

There will be ups and downs in your journey as a leader, but avoid the trap of low self-esteem. The most unhappy people in the world are those who care the most about what other people think about them. There are three opinions that matter in life:
- God's opinion of you
- Your opinion of God
- Your opinion of yourself

Solomon was another leader who depended on the divine guidance of God. Solomon's leadership style was one of commitment to fairness and justice. He was known for being a just and impartial leader, making decisions that were based on what was right, rather than what was popular or convenient. In the account of Solomon requesting wisdom from God (1 KINGS 3:1-14), we see that he already possessed a quality that was necessary for discernment and humility. He could have requested anything from God but instead, he asked for wisdom to lead the people God had placed under his reign.
- Knowledge knows what to do.
- Skill knows how to do it.
- Wisdom knows when to do or if it should be done at all.

A leader needs to be able to discern between right and wrong, good and bad. Discernment is the ability to properly discriminate or make a determination. Discernment is the mark of maturity. As a leader, you must be able to see what others don't see. Solomon demonstrated his discernment when he wisely ruled in a dispute between two mothers, over which of them was the rightful mother of a baby (1 KINGS 3:16-28).

" *So give your servant a discerning heart to govern your people and to distinguish between right and wrong.*
1 KINGS 3:9

This verse shows us that in order for us to lead others well, we must first be able to distinguish between right and wrong ourselves. This is something that only comes with a personal relationship with God and studying His word. As we grow in our relationship with Him, He begins to reveal areas of our lives that need to change. It is only through repentance and obedience to His word that we can develop the true discernment needed to lead others.

Discernment is a quality that all leaders must possess if they want to be effective in their roles. This quality allows us to see things from God's perspective and make decisions based on what is right, instead of what is popular or easy. If you are currently in a leadership role or aspire to be a leader one day, begin developing this quality by humbly submitting yourself to God and His word daily.

" *Discernment is not knowing the difference between right and wrong. It is knowing the difference between right and almost right*
CHARLES SPURGEON

As a result of divine guidance, I started my own business at a very young age. Due to a divine gift in art and music, I leveraged them both to start my journey in entrepreneurship and leadership. The first business that I started was a custom sign painting business, and later, a musician for hire, while simultaneously going to college and moonlighting as a disc jockey. While I called myself taking a break from the public, I tried what I thought would be a short break, a position with the federal government. After a short time with the federal government, I was selected to be a team lead, then a supervisor, then a manager, and the rest is history. Over 30 years later and multiple leadership/ management assignments, here I am as a management consultant.

God Made You to Be An Answer to Somebody's Problem

" *The two most important days in your life are the day you are born and the day you find out why.*
MARK TWAIN

You were made to be an answer to somebody's problem, and as a leader, you often begin walking in that gift and calling at an early age. I found myself in that role often, regardless of the people whom I worked with or served with in organizations. After years in leadership within a myriad of settings, e.g. as a Presiding Prelate of a Christian Ministry Organization, a Pastor, a Senior Manager in the Department of Defense, to a leader of a band as a musician in professional musical groups, I soon learned about the impact of sound leadership, especially as a Kingdom man—and more importantly, God had strategically placed me.

As a leader, you've been given a platform. A platform is a powerful place to be, and if you don't recognize that power, you can damage people and distort the dreams of others. A stage is for performance, but a platform is for influence. Whether you like it or not, you are an influencer, a difference maker. Leave a mark, not a scar. The things that you say to subordinates in your leadership role can provide encouragement along with constructive criticism (a mark) or lasting damage and discouragement (a scar). In scripture, God says that we should be salt and light. Let people see your light and taste your salt. The analogy is that salt seasons and makes food taste better. Your light is the leadership that you bring to show them the way, and the salt is what you should add to their character to make them not only improve in skill but become a better person.

Potential: Use What Is in Your Hand

DISCOVER YOUR GIFT, skill, or talent as a leader. It is important that young leaders and those who aspire to be leaders discover what is in their hands. The question that God asked Moses that changed everything was "What is in your hand?" It was the rod that was in his hand that God would later work through to open the Red Sea which would enable over two million people to walk through to escape captivity in Egypt. What is in your hand can open doors for you and others. It is a shame to discover your potential or ability, and then never discover why you have it.

> **"** *And Moses answered and said, But, behold, they will not believe me, nor hearken unto my voice: for they will say, The LORD hath not appeared unto thee. 2 And the LORD said unto him, What is that in thine hand? And he said, A rod.*
>
> EXODUS 4:1-3

THE DANNY SIMPSON STORY. On September 19, 1990, a 24-year-old named Danny Simpson robbed a bank in Ottawa, Canada. During the robbery, Simpson utilized a .45 caliber Colt semiautomatic to carry out his plan of demanding $6,000 from the bank. Sadly, Simpson failed to realize that his weapon of choice was worth over 20 times the amount that he stole from the local bank. It was discovered that this weapon was in fact an antique created in 1918 by the Ross Rifle Company, Quebec City and was worth approximately $100,000. In the end, Simpson was found guilty and sentenced to six years in prison.

If Simpson had known this knowledge before committing this premeditated crime, this robbery may not have occurred. This story demonstrates the importance of knowing what's in your hand, and what is already within you. If you don't understand what's in your hands, along with what you possess on the inside, it will cause you to abort your future.

Simpson didn't understand what was in his possession. If he had understood what he had inherited, he would not have been trying to rob a bank. Understand your heritage and what is in your hands.

Amazingly, George Washington Carver took peanuts and developed over 300 different products. After you consider what is in your hand, don't take it for granted. Never underestimate or devalue its worth or potential.

> **So he fed them according to the integrity of his heart; and guided them by the skillfulness of his hands.**
> PSALM 78:72

In the Bible, as a leader, David used the skill that God put in his hand to lead the people. Great leaders are great learners. Leadership potential involves showing traits, abilities, skills, and characteristics often associated with being a successful leader. Many organizations look for individuals with leadership potential, so that they can build a strong workforce and develop future leaders within the organization. Potential is about what you haven't done yet. Many are promoted on the potential seen by senior management. They are looking at who you can be and hoping that is who you will be and contribute to the organization. In the military, senior officers will tell you that most are promoted on potential. It is what you are capable of doing. Identifying leadership potential in employees and helping them develop their leadership skills offer multiple important benefits to organizations.

Real success happens over time, so there has to be a commitment to the process. There must be consistency and discipline.

Consistency and Discipline

CONSISTENCY—of the same quality every time.

DISCIPLINE—a way of behaving that shows a willingness to obey rules or orders.

- Wherever there is mastering, there is discipline.
- You must be consistent and disciplined for success.
- Some things are not a devil in the details; it is a discipline issue.

The thing that you are most passionate about will give you the most pain. Whatever your passion is will be where your greatest pain comes from. It pains you to see someone do poorly in what you are passionate about. As a musician, it pains me to hear someone playing in the wrong key. It is irritating. If a person has a gift of organization, it pains him or her to come into a cluttered workspace. As a leader, pain comes with the territory. Each level of leadership can bring a different level of pain. Some people can't physically go to higher levels because of the pressure on the mountain in those high places. Either you adapt, or you have to come down to a lower level. Again, the greatest lessons in life are not obtained in a course but on a course.

" *But ye are a chosen generation, a royal priesthood, an holy nation, a peculiar people; that ye should shew forth the praises of him who hath called you out of darkness into his marvelous light.*

1 PETER 2:9

The Jethro Leadership Principle

JETHRO'S LEADERSHIP ADVICE **was meant to benefit both Moses (CEO) and the Israelites (The Company / Organization). Without leadership, an organization has friction, confusion, and underperformance.**

EXODUS 18:13-27

13 The next day Moses took his seat to serve as judge for the people, and they stood around him from morning till evening. **14** *When his father-in-law saw all that Moses was doing for the people, he said, "What is this you are doing for the people? Why do you alone sit as judge, while all these people stand around you from morning till evening?"* **15** *Moses answered him, "Because the people come to me to seek God's will.* **16** *Whenever they have a dispute, it is brought to me, and I decide between the parties and inform them of God's decrees and instructions."* **17** *Moses' father-in-law replied, "What you are doing is not good.* **18** *You and these people who come to you will only wear yourselves out. The work is too heavy for you; you cannot handle it alone.* **19** *Listen now to me and I will give you some advice, and may God be with you. You must be the people's representative before God and bring their disputes to him.* **20** *Teach them his decrees and instructions, and show them the way they are to live and how they are to behave.* **21** *But select capable men from all the people—men who fear God, trustworthy men who hate dishonest gain—and appoint* *them as officials over thousands, hundreds, fifties and tens.* **22** *Have them serve as judges for the people at all times, but have them bring every difficult case to you; the simple cases they can decide themselves. That will make your load lighter, because they will share it with you.* **23** *If you do this and God so commands, you will be able to stand the strain, and all these people will go home satisfied.* **24** *Moses listened to his father-in-law and did everything he said.* **25** *He chose capable men from all Israel and made them leaders of the people, officials over thousands, hundreds, fifties and tens.* **26** *They served as judges for the people at all times. The difficult cases they brought to Moses, but the simple ones they decided themselves.* **27** *Then Moses sent his father-in-law on his way, and Jethro returned to his own country. (NIV)*

The Jethro Leadership Principle:
- Jethro advised Moses to teach/mentor others.
- Jethro advised Moses to appoint others as officials/managers over the people.
- Jethro advised Moses to take on only the most difficult/highest-level cases.

Advice On Type of Leaders to Select (EXODUS 18:21):
- ABLE MEN: **Competence**
- MEN THAT FEAR GOD: **Character**
- MEN OF TRUTH: **Integrity**
- HATING COVETOUSNESS: **Fair/Not Backstabbers or Envious**

Note: When hiring, you don't need someone whom you can chill with; you need someone whom you can build with.

Traits of Biblical leaders who finished well in life:
- Humility
- Intimacy with God
- Obedience
- Faith
- Ability to receive counsel

***Moses received counsel and mentorship from his father-in-law and finished well.**

The potential of your organization rests on the strength of the people:
- Don't just find great leaders; build great leaders.
- Realize that there's untapped potential all around you.
- If you delegate authority, you will develop leaders.
- Goals don't determine success; the systems you put in place determine success.
- Properly placed people prevent problems.
- Improperly placed people cause problems.

❝ *It's not a person's accomplishments that make them great, it's who they surround themselves with.*
GEN NORMAN SCHWARZKOPF

Character Is Key

OFTEN, GOD ALLOWS you to grow slowly and go through the process of becoming a leader. Slow success builds character; fast success builds ego. Fame comes in a moment, but greatness comes over time. Character is defined as the way someone thinks, feels, and behaves; qualities of honesty, courage, or the like; integrity. Your gift or skill can take you to high places, but it is your character that will keep you there. You can be skilled and gifted enough to get there but not mature enough to stay. This is why some leaders, politicians, entertainers, entrepreneurs, and athletes don't last long. Success and fame came before they developed the character to sustain it. Your attitude, words unwisely spoken, and arrogance can kill your career. Character is both revealed and developed by tests. Many times, God will test you in a low place before He can trust you in a high place. In management, some keys to good character makeup are emotional intelligence (EI) and adaptability quotient (AQ), which are a big part of your ability to lead. EI is the ability to stay calm in a crisis and still respond with wisdom. EI is important in leadership because it improves self-awareness, increases accountability, and builds trusting relationships by helping leaders process their emotions in a more positive way, which allows them to address challenges more effectively. AQ is the ability to adapt to change. A person's AQ will not only determine how he or she will thrive personally in the rapidly changing environment and modernization, but also play a significant role in how effectively he or she can lead others through these times of rapidly changing technology and increasingly chaotic times. You need good character for both EI and AQ to sustain your success.

How you spend your time is determined by your character. To make a difference, you can't follow the crowd. When you follow the crowd, you get no farther than the crowd. Average is simply being on top of the bottom. You can't do here what you did there. As you observe a person with good character, check how that person spends his or her time and money. Look at the person's calendar, and it will denote character. Your priorities expose and reveal your character. How you interact with people and show compassion with fairness are traits of character, as well.

Why is Character Important to Your Success?

Leadership creates moments not defined by policy or procedures. There are situations when leaders have to choose between right and almost right. Every day, you make character decisions, consciously or unconsciously, such as between speed or quality and long-term or short-term results. The impact of these decisions either reinforces your team's desired or undesired thoughts, feelings, and behaviors.

Leadership character is demonstrated to align the leader-follower relationship, increasing both leader and follower productivity, effectiveness, and creativity. Leadership character plays a vital role in unifying a team.

A focus on helping others is essential to providing effective strategic leadership because followers will give more when they respect the leader's character. Also, character helps leaders navigate change more effectively.

What is Leadership Character?
Leadership character is doing the right thing for the right reasons and with the right intentions. It is the inner heart of leadership.

Five key leadership character principles:
- INTEGRITY—Being honest, acting consistently with principles, standing up for what is right, and keeping promises. Doing the right thing when nobody is looking.
- RESPONSIBILITY—Owning personal decisions, admitting mistakes, and showing concern for the common good.
- FORGIVENESS—Letting go of self and others' mistakes, focused on what is right versus only what is wrong.
- COMPASSION—Empathizing with others, empowering others, actively caring for others, and committing to others' growth.
- ACCOUNTABILITY—Surrounding yourself with accountability partners. Share the list of principles that you have defined, and invite people close enough who know you well to hold you accountable if you start to get off track. Leaders tend to become more isolated as they move higher in a company, and the role of a coach and mentor becomes even more critical.

Practicing these five principles will help you build character. You must know and understand the non-negotiables. A leader's character determines how knowledge, skills, and abilities are applied. Leadership decisions are often based on values, worldviews, and past experiences. Your past, even as a child, has shaped your current perception of what is right or wrong. Family members, business partners, friends, religious leaders, and the community where you live and work reinforce your character. Refuse to lower your standards because you are around people who refuse to raise theirs. If they refuse to raise their standard, don't lower yours.

> **❝** *The ultimate measure of a man is not where he stands in moments of convenience and comfort, but where he stands at times of challenge and controversy.*
> MARTIN LUTHER KING, JR.

Leadership and Integrity

INTEGRITY IN LEADERSHIP means doing the right thing when nobody's looking or simply having strong, moral principles and standing by your words. It's a highly valued trait since most employees look to their leader to demonstrate and set the standard on how to conduct themselves. Leaders with integrity demonstrate a clear set of beliefs that guide their direction, actions, and decision-making. Power and authority have to come with integrity. Authority is given by the integrity of your heart and the skill of your hand. Authority is willfully given because people respect you. Our Lord, Jesus Christ in His kingdom leadership demonstrated these principles above all. These principles can develop early in a leader's career or as part of a person's upbringing. Having a clear set of principles that are apparent to everyone helps your colleagues know your position on an issue and anticipate your reaction to a situation. Leaders who demonstrate organizational values in their actions help set expectations for acceptable behavior. Whatever is not evaluated cannot be improved. You can have competence without integrity, but you can't have integrity without competence. Demonstrating high ethical standards of conduct also promotes a positive work culture that motivates others in your organization, subordinates, and employees in general to do their best and increases their loyalty to the organization. Leaders with integrity are trustworthy. When I was in Army Management Staff

College, I wrote a white paper entitled "Trust, the Missing Army Value." I believe all of the United States Army values swing on the hinges of trust. In a challenging situation, leaders with integrity remain committed to their beliefs. Standing by these beliefs can guide leaders in their decision-making to help their team towards a course of action. Leaders who stay consistent in their beliefs give employees confidence in their decisions, which leads to stability within an organization. Trustworthy leaders do what they say they're going to do. They've shown their desire to seek input from others to make more informed decisions. Colleagues have confidence in their judgment and ability to be truthful about a situation.

> **"** *A true leader has the confidence to stand alone, the courage to make tough decisions, and the compassion to listen to the needs of others. He does not set out to be a leader, but becomes one by the equality of his actions and the integrity of his intent.*
> DOUGLAS MACARTHUR

Trustworthy managers also extend their trust to the people whom they lead. They demonstrate confidence in their team's capabilities and support them in their efforts. This trust encourages employees to do their best work. Leaders with integrity tell the truth despite the consequences. This is Kingdom Leadership at its best. Honesty helps prevent smaller problems from becoming a detriment to an organization.

Being honest also helps earn the trust of others in the organization whom you work for. This can be important in building relationships with your team members. Being truthful shows that you respect the other person, which can improve your future working relationships.

❝ *The supreme quality for leadership is unquestionable integrity. Without it, no real success is possible, no matter whether it is on a section gang, a football field, in an army, or in an office.*
DWIGHT D. EISENHOWER, former five-star Army General and U.S. President

❝ *Integrity is the most important characteristic of a leader, and one that he or she must be prepared to demonstrate again and again.*
WARREN BENNIS

❝ *I look for three things in hiring people. The first is personal integrity, the second is intelligence, and the third is high energy level. But if you don't have the first, the other two will kill you.*
WARREN BUFFETT

Integrity and Skill. Godly leadership requires integrity and skill. In corporate America, you must have integrity. You want someone who is both nice and competent. Whether you work in a corporation or the church, you need to have skill and a heart of integrity. Leadership is about serving others, not your own selfish interest. It takes a heart of integrity to understand this. As previously stated, when hiring and selecting leaders, you don't need someone whom you can chill with; you need someone whom you can build with. It is a dangerous thing to have leaders who have skills with no integrity.

When in trouble or a tough situation, most will ask, "How do I get out of this?" The person with skill and integrity of heart will ask, "What do I get out of this?" not "How do I get out of this?" "What can I learn from this?" You don't just go through it; grow through it.

Humility in Leadership

HUMILITY IS A key quality to sound Kingdom Leadership. The American Psychological Association defines humility as, "characterized by a low focus on the self, an accurate (not over- or underestimated) sense of one's accomplishments and worth, and an acknowledgment of one's limitations, imperfections, mistakes, gaps in knowledge, and so on" (*APA Dictionary of Psychology*, n.d.).

To make it much simpler, humility is not thinking less of yourself, but less about yourself and more about others. Essentially, you recognize your strengths and successes, but you also understand your weaknesses and limitations. In the Kingdom, God says, "Humble yourselves therefore under the mighty hand of God, that He may exalt you in due time" (1 PETER 5:6). He also states, "Whosoever exalts himself shall be abased, and he that humbles himself shall be exalted" (LUKE 14:11). As a leader, these scriptures can be vitally helpful. You don't assume that you always have the answer or know the best way forward. Leading with assumptions can have a negative impact on your organization, business, and team. Instead, as a humble leader, you recognize when and where you may need help or outside input. There is no one-size-fits-all approach to humility in leadership. However, there are certain qualities that humble leaders tend to have in common, including:

- **A desire to learn.** Because humble leaders don't over-inflate their own abilities, they recognize that there's always more to learn in life and leadership. This student mentality means that they're always looking to grow and learn new things, and that a culture of learning often trickles down to their team or organization.

- **The ability to reveal what they don't know.** It's one thing to want to learn and be okay with making mistakes, but for leaders, it's equally important to set the climate in the workplace, make that visible, and model it for their teams. Humble leaders aren't afraid to show vulnerability and say, "I don't know." They realize that this is why we have a team, a staff, skilled subordinates, and partners. To be more effective, the humble leader has learned to ask the right questions that frame the problem and draw out new information.

- **Solid listening skills.** Humble leaders are aware that there is plenty that they don't know. They are typically more sincere with a willingness to listen to other people and consider their ideas. You will learn more about effective listening in a follow-on chapter of this book.

- **A focus on collaboration.** Humble leaders recognize their limitations. They know that to overcome those limitations, they'll need to work with other people. Not only does this make them more open to receiving feedback, but it also fosters a collaborative spirit across their teams. This type of collaboration at work can lead to better outcomes, e.g. increased innovation, improved team performance, and a more positive working environment. This is even more important with virtual teams, which we see more of today and have become a norm in some organizations.

- **More authenticity.** Humble leaders have a clear understanding of who they are, what they bring to the table, and the areas that present growth opportunities. They are more authentic. They are not trying to act like they have any flaws or weaknesses. When authenticity is modeled from the top down, it changes the entire work environment, fostering esprit de corps and camaraderie in the workplace.

- **A compassionate leadership style.** Humble leaders recognize the fact that they're not perfect. They recognize that their team members are not perfect either and don't expect them to be. They bring a sense of care and compassion to their management style and allow space for their teams to learn, grow, and make mistakes.

- **A willingness to admit when they're wrong.** Although they strive for perfection, humble leaders recognize that they're capable of getting it wrong and have no problem admitting it when they do.

Humility in leadership can manifest in different ways in different people. However, at the core, it's about recognizing that being a leader doesn't make you invincible, and that you, like every other person, have areas where you can grow, change, and improve. When you are done learning, you're done. It is as simple as that. Some people are born with humility. If that's you, chances are, humility in leadership comes naturally. On the contrary, if you're not a person who has natural humility, you're going to have to work on that part of your character and actively infuse humility into your leadership style.

> *Do nothing out of selfish ambition or vain conceit. Rather, in humility value others above yourselves.*
> PHILIPPIANS 2:3 (NIV)

Why Humility Is Essential In Leadership?

Humility is an important skill when you're in a leadership role. Why, exactly, is it so essential? Humility is more than just a skill; it has to be a part of you. There are a number of reasons why humility is one of the most important leadership competencies:

- **It makes you more accessible and relatable to your team.** No one wants to approach an arrogant leader. When you embrace humility in leadership, it makes you more approachable and accessible to your team. Additionally, it fosters an atmosphere and climate where subordinates can be open and honest, producing a reality of true success as opposed to phony success that's built upon lies.

- **It helps you innovate.** Humble leaders are more open to others' creativity, insights, and ideas. When you can appreciate and build on others' ideas and creativity, you generate better solutions and increase innovation.

- **It helps you gain influence.** In the workplace, humility is attractive. According to the **Harvard Business Review**:
  Humble leaders improve the performance of a company in the long run because they create more collaborative environments. They have a balanced view of themselves—both their virtues and shortcomings—and a strong appreciation of others' strengths and contributions, while being open to new ideas and feedback.
  (MAYO PARA. 2).
  When leaders maintain a posture of humility, it causes employees and team members to have a greater sense of respect for their leader. This leads to a transformed dynamic in the workplace that creates less resistance to authority and causes the leader's influence to grow exponentially by reaching individuals inside and outside the workplace.

- **It leads to better outcomes.** According to a research study published in *The Journal of Management*, it is highly recommended that organizations and businesses utilize "humility as a criterion of executive selection and that human resource managers target humility in executive coaching" (Ou et al., 2015, p. 1167). Moreover, organizations that face calamity or extreme losses are often due to executive leadership who lack humility (Ou et al., 2015, p. 1167). Humble leadership increases productivity, employee morale, collaborative partnerships, and organizational success.

" *Humble yourselves before the Lord, and he will lift you up.*
JAMES 4:10 (NIV)

Bottom line: Humility in leadership is important because it makes you a better leader.
- Humble leaders ask for help and don't pretend to know everything.
- Humble leaders admit mistakes and forgive mistakes.
- Humble leaders adopt a growth mindset and are open to new ideas.
- Humble leaders put the needs of their team first.
- Humble leaders model inclusive leadership.
- Humble leaders recognize and celebrate their employees.

" *Therefore, as God's chosen people, holy and dearly loved, clothe yourselves with compassion, kindness, humility, gentleness and patience. Bear with each other and forgive one another if any of you has a grievance against someone. Forgive as the Lord forgave you.*
COLOSSIANS 3:12-13 (NIV)

The Importance of People Skills

SOME PEOPLE ARE technically sound but lack leadership skills. Just because someone has the skill set to do the job, it does not mean that he or she can lead people. This is one of the biggest mistakes in leadership. Sometimes that person will also be your biggest problem if leadership skills are not exhibited. This opens the door to counterproductive leadership. Counterproductive leadership is the abuse of authority that inflicts serious harm on followers and the organization. These are the employees who say one thing upstairs and another thing downstairs. If you are not careful with this important leadership nugget, your organization can be destroyed from the bottom up. Great Leadership has **PEOPLE SKILLS FIRST.**

Why do I need people skills to be an effective leader? Let's discuss this problem. In most professions, secular and sacred job roles, you need to have a good level of people skills. When you become a leader, it's important to reflect on the skills that you've learned previously and develop them to become the best version of yourself. Bad people skills can result in conflicts in the organization and the potential of losing valuable team members. To put it bluntly, to be a good leader, it is imperative that you have good people skills. The risks of poor communication from leaders should be avoided at all costs. If you have good people skills, your employees will more than likely be able to relate to you, leading to stronger relationships and trust in the workplace. Good people skills have the power to positively change the atmosphere in the workplace. A *Harvard Business Review* survey reported that 58% of people would trust a complete stranger more than their own boss (Sturt & Nordstrom, 2018). Today, this means there is much work to do.

Let's start with the most important people skill:
- **RESPECT.** No one wants to work for someone who does not treat him or her with respect. As human beings, we should treat others the way that we want to be treated, as this principle should not change in the workplace. According to the *Harvard Business Review*, disrespect in the workplace is shockingly common in the 21st century, as approximately 98% of employees in 2019 experienced varied types of disrespect within the span of that year (Taylor et al., 2019). Leaders who operate from a foundation of respect are more likely to succeed in times of crisis, which leads to a higher likelihood of longer organizational sustainability (Oak Engage, 2022).
- **PATIENCE.** Patience is the ability to wait for something without complaining about the amount of time it may take to occur. As a result, patience is vital within the workplace. Maintaining a patient attitude can help prevent employees from experiencing frustration and burnout (Oak Engage, 2022). Always ensure that you remain patient in any circumstance, as someone was once patient with you. Therefore, reciprocate the same treatment that you would want someone to show towards you.
- **EMPATHY.** Empathy is the ability to share and understand someone else's feelings, experiences, and emotions. A study conducted by *Oak Engage Business Solutions*, found that 92%

of employees agree that empathetic leadership is directly correlated with high rates of employee retention (2022). Overall, employees want to feel heard and understood. All leaders should strive to demonstrate empathy as a way to show their employees that they care and value them as people.

- **SMILE.** A smile from a leader to a subordinate employee on a seemingly hectic or difficult day is extremely powerful. During the 1970's, a young man in his thirties committed suicide by jumping off the Golden Gate Bridge. Although this bridge has been a prominent place where many people have committed suicides, the story with this young man was different from the rest. During the investigation, the medical examiner went to the deceased man's residence and found a letter. The letter said, "I'm going to walk to the bridge. If one person smiles at me on the way, I will not jump" (Greenhouse, 2014).

After putting the pieces of the puzzle together, it can be inferred that he did not receive a smile from a single person, as the end result was suicide. Could you imagine walking several blocks and not receiving a single hello, how are you, or a smile from anyone?

As leaders, we should always maintain a positive demeanor, and most importantly, smile. I understand that we may become preoccupied with business and personal life endeavors, or even have a challenging day, but we must always watch our demeanor, as our demeanor sets the atmosphere in the organization. Well, one may ask how do you initiate a positive atmosphere? The answer is a simple, smile.

Smiling is like laughter, as it can bring joy, uplift one's mood, establish hope, and create a positive environment. Always remember, smiles are free, so have two or three.

❝ *If you want to improve the organization, you have to improve yourself, and the organization gets pulled up with you.*
INDRA NOOYI

Managing the Manager

IN SHORT, MANAGING the manager is simply understanding what your manager wants, how he or she wants it, and the specifics of how the manager likes it. For example, if the manager says he/she wants the slides outlined in blue, don't come into his or her office with them outlined in red. Managing the manager is a tool that, when utilized wisely, can control the mood of the manager. Some would say it is simply giving the manager what he/she wants. However, to go further, it enables you to build a great team culture, cultivate strong relationships, be aligned on goals and expectations, stay engaged in the work, and create a better environment between you as a leader and your manager for accountability. This is actually learning on a greater level and potentially experiencing exponential growth. The critical difference is that the project you're overseeing and supporting is not just the task, but also the manager. Sounds simple, but managing the manager is tricky because it's both a technical and a relational skill. When managing the manager, you're paying attention to the outcomes that your team/staff achieves and how you relate to your manager. In traditional hierarchical structures, the manager/staff relationship has a built-in power dynamic. That's what we call discrete positional power—it's part of your job to manage the manager but to also help your manager hold the power responsibly. This includes seeking to understand how the manager's other identities (age, race, gender, etc.) and experiences with power and privilege intersect with his or her role at work.

Managing the manager requires familiarity not just with management best practices, adaptability and responsiveness, and keen attention to equity and inclusion, but the manager's personal best practices.

Here are four tips for managing the manager:

1. **Cultivate and affirm the management relationship.** One common challenge for many subordinate managers is "cultivating" their relationship with management. Cultivating the management relationship means embracing the responsibility that comes with positional power and growing the relationship as you learn more about leadership. In most workplaces, positional power gives a manager real influence over the employees' quality of life at work, i.e. how much they're paid, how they receive feedback, opportunities for advancement, their sense of belonging, and sometimes beyond (references for future jobs). These decisions require context (including knowledge of policies) and a sense of responsibility for one's authority. Additionally, when you're a manager, you're not just on the hook for your performance and your work; you're responsible for supporting someone else. This requires skill in coaching, delegating, and holding others accountable, where a manager's approach can shape staff experience. Finally, managing the manager can also have an impact on stress levels, emotional health, and one's sense of belonging, which is even more complicated when managing across lines of difference. While many managers struggle with owning

their management, authority, and influence, the "why" behind it may vary. Here are some possible reasons:

- Lack of confidence that comes with being in a new role.
- Growing pains associated with a promotion (especially if the person is now managing their peers).
- Feelings of doubt exacerbated by bias and exclusion at interpersonal, organizational, and systemic levels.
- Feeling nervous about having power and influence and not wanting to make a mistake.

Managers benefit from the time invested to cultivate and affirm ownership over their sphere of influence, which is a core competency for their role.

2. **Understand the management and leadership style.** Managers should reflect on and share their management and leadership styles as part of the "getting to know you" portion of onboarding and developing relationships with new staff. This insight is also helpful for managing the manager because it gives you a sense of their strengths and how you might support them. For example, if they are a big-picture thinker who doesn't tend to focus on details, they may be more likely to leave out important information when delegating assignments to their staff. As a subordinate manager, you might offer to help them prepare for delegation conversations by asking them for time to talk you through the assignments.

3. **Observe the manager in action.** Find ways to see your manager in the act of managing:
   - Observe team meetings.
   - Watch and listen to feedback.
   - Observe the approach to site visits.
   - Observe conduct job interviews.
   - Pay attention to feedback on performance evaluations.

The purpose of observing or shadowing the manager is to help you better understand his or her management and leadership style. It is an opportunity for you to learn from the manager and model management styles. Pay attention to how things are performed differently from you and appreciate those differences.

4. **Build a professional relationship with your manager.** Building authentic respectful and appropriate relationships with the manager has four significant benefits: First, it gives you a better sense of what's happening in the company or organization. Second, when the manager knows you, he or she is more likely to approach you and share more insight on a problem. Third, it makes it easier to develop trust. Finally, a strong professional relationship with your manager can lead to a stronger, more cohesive team, and a greater sense of belonging.

The Power of Mentorship

MENTORSHIP REFERS TO a personal developmental relationship in which a more experienced or more knowledgeable person helps a less experienced or less knowledgeable person. Wise people will sharpen you. I heard a wise leader say, "If you want to know your future, look at who you run with."

Your closest friends often shape your:
- Values
- Direction
- Life

❝ *He that walketh with wise men shall be wise: but a companion of fools shall be destroyed.*
PROVERBS 13:20

Your choices determine your:
- Conduct
- Character
- Destiny

Mentorship can provide numerous benefits for mentors and their mentees. Developing this relationship can help both groups to learn new things, build networks, and grow as professionals. Mentoring is super important for leaders because simply put, it brings the best out of the people whom you lead. Mentoring generates confidence, inspires trust, and fast-tracks team development. Mentoring is something that can be done successfully by anybody in a position of experience. The role of the mentor is basically to nurture the mentee, by providing encouragement to learn, grow, and upskill. This empowers the mentee to not only perform better in his or her role but also experience career progression.

Mentors encourage and enable another person's professional or personal development. A mentor can help focus efforts by setting goals and giving feedback. As a result, companies that want to build employees' skills often create mentoring programs. The mentors' knowledge can help train and create a high-quality and productive workforce. Employees appreciate workplaces that encourage development, as it can demonstrate that their employer values them and wants to see them grow. A mentor can help the mentee set personal or professional development goals. For effective goal-setting and accountability, the mentor can create SMART goals—specific, measurable, achievable, relevant, and time-based. These goals can help focus the mentee's efforts and make it easier for the mentor to track and assess progress. The mentor may identify smaller tasks in pursuit of a larger objective to develop specific skills or meet particular priorities. A mentor helps to hold his or her mentee accountable for achieving goals. By tracking progress, the mentor helps the mentee stay focused and on track toward completing them. It can also ensure that the mentee does not forget about the goals that have been set. Knowing that someone else is watching can serve as motivation, as the mentee likely does not want to disappoint the mentor by failing to meet goals. This encouragement can motivate the mentee to keep moving forward despite challenges.

Trust represents a core element in mentoring relationships. The mentee must trust that the mentor has his or her best interests in mind and will provide accurate and honest guidance. The business world can be competitive, so the mentee needs to rely on a trusted mentor to keep confidential information private when necessary. Communicating regularly and following through on promises demonstrate two methods of establishing trust in these relationships. A mentor can help build the mentee's professional network. When the mentee identifies professional or personal goals, the mentor can connect him or her to potential opportunities or individuals who can help. As the mentor typically has more industry experience or a higher-level career, these connections can be valuable for career advancement. A trusting mentorship relationship enables honest feedback. By establishing trust, the mentee understands that constructive criticism aims to build professional growth rather than demean. Sometimes the secret to progress is not something that we need to learn but something that we need to remember and apply. Mentors can identify weaknesses and advise on ways to improve. Because this is a professional relationship, the mentor plays an objective role. Meanwhile, a friend may hesitate to identify the mentee's weaknesses to avoid appearing critical. When possible, individuals should choose mentors who have the experience relevant to their profession or goals. When mentors convey their successes, the mentees can model their example and emulate the steps that they took. Mentors can also share the mistakes that they made along their journey. The mentees benefit because they learn lessons about the mistakes' negative impacts but do not have to suffer the consequences themselves. Learning about these experiences can also help prepare the mentees for the challenges that they can expect to face and receive advice on how to overcome them.

Fight in Your Weight Class

MANY LEADERS GET in trouble fighting above or below their weight class. For example, a flyweight boxer will frustrate a heavyweight boxer. The heavyweight boxer will end up chasing the flyweight boxer around the ring. The two are not in the same weight class. You never fight outside your weight class, whether above or below. Either one can spell trouble. Why is a Colonel going toe-to-toe with a private first-class soldier? Why is the CEO or Director going toe-to-toe with an entry-level employee? Senior leaders lead through subordinate leaders.

To provide context, weight divisions are defined to ensure that fair conditions are in place during the match between two opponents. These conditions also ensure that mismatches are prevented and that the environment is safe for the opponents (Rusth, 2022). Currently, the 17 weight classes in men's professional boxing ranging from 'strawweight (105 lbs.)' to 'heavyweight (200 plus lbs.)' assist with upholding fair conditions (Rusth, 2022).

When opponents are close to the same weight, the determining factor in the outcome of the match is usually skill, not size. However, size can still be a factor. If two opponents are evenly matched and one is slightly bigger than the other, that person may have an advantage. This is also true in an executive boardroom.

Likewise, always ensure that the leaders you have at the executive table are equally ranked. When you are in your weight class, you generally speak to each other on a first-name basis. When individuals at the table are equally ranked, the fight is fair, and no one is in fear of speaking up. In instances when you are outranked, speaking up could kill your career in cases where someone feels that you are targeting or exposing him or her in a manner that is unfavorable. For example, the Colonel may be afraid to speak up and stand his ground at the table with General Officers unless he or she has an ally at the table who gives him or her space to speak. The right answer at the wrong time is the wrong answer. Always fight in your weight class, and delegate to the next manager or officer. As a key reminder, always respect those above you. This principle, as they say in show business, could make or break your career.

Let the Game Come to You!

HOW MANY COACHES have counseled anxious and pressing players and told them, "Let the game come to you." It's hard advice; even odd advice in a world of sports and professions where aggression and taking control are the preferred strategies. "Getting there first" or "controlling the tempo" in the face of this disciplined approach can be a challenge, yet this sage and prowess advice matters profoundly for successful athletic and professional endeavors. *Letting the game come to you*, however, takes discipline, strong virtue, and character in order to learn these skills and insight. Notice that the advice begins with the notion of a "game." A game presumes a goal; participants know what they want to achieve and do so in a competitive environment. Usually, the athletes and professionals work with a team to achieve the end result. Many new leaders and managers think that they have to start making changes right away to establish the facts or make a statement that they are the boss. That is one of the major mistakes of new managers and leaders. As in sports, we need to adhere to this wise cliché that says, "Let the game come to you." In other words, take time to assess the climate, and execute your role and your responsibility at your level, "let the game come to you." Another way of stating it is, once it is elevated to you, examine the facts and/or analysis first, and then execute with the authority that you have, making an educated decision, to make change and win.

In management, don't try to fix what's not broken. This unwise decision can upset harmony amongst your team and inadvertently affect efficiency and effectiveness. Changing a process or action because you have the authority, just because you can, is a sign of immaturity and is indicative of the fact that you don't really know your purpose and who you are. I've seen this many times in the changing of policy, programs, and processes over the course of my many years in leadership roles. Make changes that enhance people and represent the Kingdom of God. Success is not something that you achieve; it is something that you attract by who you have become. It is important to understand why you have the gift that you have. Make a difference!

The Wisdom of Listening

THE WISDOM OF listening in leadership is crucial for team performance. The real art of communication is not in your ability to speak but in your ability to listen.

- Be quick to listen, slow to speak (JAMES 1:19).
- In leadership, listen and assess up front before making decisions.
- Don't be hasty to change things before understanding the "why."

Many things you will find out are not by opening your mouth, but simply by listening. This is especially true for a new manager or leader. Don't start making changes until you listen and understand how things operate, and ensure that you know the "why." Why do they do it that way? Why is this the process? Why is it policy? The lack of listening can lead to counterproductive leadership, team dysfunction, and poor productivity. Listening is one of the most powerful tools that you possess as a leader. It helps you not only to gain insight but build trust and foster loyalty. It informs others that they are important to you and that you value what they have to say. Unfortunately, many leaders don't carry this care nor awareness and never learn how to effectively listen. The busier you are, the more quiet time you need. Here are seven ways that the wisdom of listening makes you a more effective leader:

1. **Listening increases your capacity as a leader.** We can always learn from those around us, including those we directly report

to. Effective listening gives you knowledge and perspectives that increase your leadership capacity. Being open to feedback and new ideas from your team helps you learn and grow as a leader.

2. **Listening shows that you care.** Really listening to someone shows that you care about what they're saying and empathize with their feelings. This creates a work environment of trust. Having the trust of your employees gives you greater influence over them. At the same time, it makes them more motivated and committed to their work.

3. **Listening helps you to comprehend the situation.** If you fail to pay attention to what your employees say, you will not fully understand them or the situation.
   Failing to comprehend the situation may lead you to give advice or recommendations that are ineffective or don't get to the root of the problem.

4. **Listening helps you better understand your organization.** Listening to your employees is the best way to understand the needs of them, your clients, and your business. This helps you plan effective strategies that are oriented to the demands of your business.

5. **Listening gives you a vision of the reality on the ground.** Listening gives you knowledge and insights into the day-to-day reality of your employees. It's essential to create an atmosphere of trust and encourage your coworkers to speak openly about their daily challenges. You might be surprised at how different their reality is from your perception of it.

6. **Listening willfully helps you gain perspective.** You should never be too busy to listen. Anyone can add value to your world if you're willing to listen. How many times have you dismissed

someone because of his or her situation or title when what you should have done was listen? Wisdom doesn't just come from peers and those above you—it can come from anywhere at any time, but only if you're willing to listen. Expand your sphere of influence, and learn from those with different perspectives and experiences—you'll be glad you did.

7. **Listening to non-verbals promotes truth.** People say as much (if not more) with their actions, inactions, body language, facial expressions, etc., as they do with their verbal communication. This is one reason why face-to-face meetings are better and produce more honesty than online meetings. Sometimes body language speaks louder than words. Don't be duped into thinking that because someone isn't saying something they're not communicating. In fact, most people won't overtly verbalize opposition or disagreement, but they will almost always deliver a very clear message with their non-verbal actions.

Asking the Right Questions

GOOD LEADERS UNDERSTAND the importance and power of asking the right questions. I could always tell if I had the right people in certain executive meetings by the questions that they asked. It takes skill and knowledge to ask the right questions and get the right answers. When you need answers, ask questions. Ask honestly, respectfully, and ask patiently. The best salesmen are those who ask questions and understand the needs of the client. A consultant cannot help a client without asking a series of questions. Before you go on a job interview, ask questions about the company. The reason why some businesses fail is that they are answering the questions that nobody's asking. The only way to know the needs of the customer is to ask the right questions. This is why arrogant know-it-alls turn people off in the corporate world. You cannot teach people a lesson who think they already know. You measure people's intelligence by the quality of their questions. There is power in being able to ask the right questions. Questions enable you to understand background and root causes. Until you define the questions, you will not recognize the answers. The real art of conversation is not only to say the right thing at the right time but not to say the wrong thing at the tempting moment. The right answer spoken at the wrong time is the wrong answer. It is important to restrain your tongue from speaking what shouldn't be said. Never show your entire hand at one time. Timing is important. It is possible to do the right thing the wrong way.

Your future is shaped by the quality of questions that you ask, i.e. "Should I work with this organization? Should I hire this person? Should I invest in this technology? Will this decision compromise my integrity or my character?" The questions raise your awareness, and awareness is the beginning of change. You can't change what you are not aware of. In the Bible, God asked Adam, "Where are you (GENESIS 3:9)?" God is omniscient, and He didn't ask the question because He didn't know where Adam was, but His question brought awareness to Adam that he was out of position. Ask questions, and be prepared to adjust and change based on what you learn.

“ *The measure of intelligence is the ability to change.*
ALBERT EINSTEIN

Key questions to ask yourself as a leader:
* Who am I?
* Why am I here? It is imperative that you know the "why."
* What am I doing for others? Know your mission.
* What are my gifts and talents? *"A man's gift makes room for him and brings him before great men."* PROVERBS 18:16
* Where am I going? Know the objective and goal.
* What are my obstacles?
* How can I improve?
* How much time do I have?

Ask yourself, "What do I bring to the fight when I walk into the room? What do I bring into the room? (Peace, calm, chaos, solutions, problems, a storm, confusion, knowledge, integrity, wisdom, etc.) Am I the missing piece?"

Review Your Performance:
- What did I do well?
- What needs improvement?
- What do I need to stop doing?
- What do I need to start doing?
- Who did I help today?
- What do I wish people understood better about me?
- What was I doing when I was winning?

At the end of the day ask yourself, "What went right, what went wrong, and how can I make it better?"

Paying Attention to Detail

I HAVE OFTEN heard people negatively assess someone's ability to think strategically and see the big picture if the person comes across as one with strong attention to detail. Intuitively, this has never resonated with me, and it prompted me to dig a little deeper. More and more, I hear successful entrepreneurs and leaders talk about their obsession with detail. Attention to detail is a crucial skill for leaders because it is a source of insight. The greatest insight comes from our ability to observe, pay attention, and connect the dots. Not being able to discern some small but critical details leads to losing valuable information and being unable to quite understand why something does not work. Attention to detail can be extremely important when it comes to running a business. Things to consider as it pertains to details:

- Recognizing Counterfeit Money.
  Discernment is in the details.
- The Fine Print in a contract can help you or hurt you.
  Destruction happens in the dark.

Leaders play an important role, so it makes sense that attention to detail should be important to them, too. Attention to detail and the ability to see a project as a whole are some of the most required skills in leadership. However, not everyone sees both. In fact, more often than not, leaders need to be visionaries first, in order to see paths that no one else can. Their job is to lead the team on the right path and think about the small stuff on the way. However, if you want to really make a difference and become a truly great leader, you must learn to include the little things in your vision. Yes, it may feel a bit restrictive, but the results are worth the detour. Moreover, it's crucial to know that not every small detail is important.

Attention to detail is your ability to efficiently allocate your cognitive resources to achieve thoroughness and accuracy when accomplishing tasks, no matter how small or large. Developing strong attention to detail makes you more effective in the workplace, increasing your productivity and reducing the likelihood of error. Because attention to detail and quality of work are often closely linked, it is a skill that is desirable for companies. Obtaining strong attention to detail requires practice and the implementation of a few key strategies. A leader's reputation is important because it influences the people around him or her. Attention to detail can be a factor that impacts your reputation because it says something about you. Attention to detail is the ability to focus on all areas of a project or task, no matter how small. People with excellent attention to detail are thorough in reviewing their work. As a result, the work is generally more accurate and free of errors. For example, if you fail to pay attention to the details of an important document or presentation that you're delivering, it may unknowingly contain mistakes. Therefore, if it doesn't look like you've reviewed your work before it goes out into the world, what are you telling executives who are recipients? Your reputation is on the line.

PIE Theory

AS A YOUNG leader and manager, I attended special training administered by the Department of the Army called Personnel Management for Executives (PME). First, I attended PME 1, and two years later PME 2, which was the way the program was designed. After my attendance, the PME Program Manager contacted me and explained how they were impressed by my interaction during the course. As a result, I was asked to come back and operate in the assigned role of Resource Staff Member. This was an honor. During that time, the program invited a speaker by the name of Harvey Coleman. Mr. Coleman taught the group about the *PIE Theory*, which stands for Performance, Image, and Exposure. This theory, along with his guidance, enhanced my career and propelled my leadership ability. He explained how he hit a glass ceiling as a young employee seeking a promotion to the higher ranks of the organization that employed him. Consequently, this prompted Mr. Coleman to leave the company. After leaving his job, he was determined to discover why he could not overcome the glass ceiling that he encountered. This led him to the research that birthed the *PIE Theory*. Upon the culmination of interviewing executives at a few Fortune 500 companies, he discovered that once you reach a certain level of leadership, your performance was only about 10% of the criterion for promotion due to companies understanding that performance was how many individuals achieved their prior promotions up to that point. As a result, image (how you carried yourself, ability to speak clearly and intelligently, well groomed, and appropriate dress) was now about 30% of the decision. Finally, exposure (how well you are known by senior officials or executives at the top of the organization) was valued at 60%. For more senior positions, senior leaders are more comfortable with those whom they have been exposed to. The decisions of higher-level leaders have a greater impact. Therefore, senior leaders and CEOs are more apt to select individuals for senior-level positions whom they know, or who are recommended by individuals whom they know, due to the existing exposure that they have had with those individuals. According to Mr. Coleman, exposure is about 60% of the criteria used for promotion to senior levels. I have shared the *PIE Theory* with many over the years, and I have built upon it as you will discover in this book. Therefore, I am sharing this powerful leadership theory by Mr. Coleman with you. Here is how the *PIE Theory* works:

- **PERFORMANCE: 10%—You must perform exceptionally well.** To receive the next promotion, you must be in the top tier. Be sure that you have a performance plan, which you work through with your manager. This plan should contain objectives that you will meet during the year and should be specific, measurable, and directly tied to the bottom line of the organization. You should also make sure that there is a degree of difficulty involved to ensure your manager knows that you are capable of more responsibility. If you are having difficulty during the year, be sure to ask for help or clarification because remember, your next promotion is on the line (Agwai, 2023).

- **IMAGE: 30%—Cultivate the proper image.** First-class work may get you a ticket for admission to the Promotion

Meeting, but you are not there yet. As we are learning, great performance is not enough. Next, you must manage your image. This includes things like verbal and non-verbal communication, dress, facial hair, teamwork, and attitude. You must look and act the part of your next promotion. What does your boss wear on "Casual Fridays"? How does your boss display disagreement? Look throughout the organization and find a mentor. Find someone who can help you develop your image and provide feedback as to how you are viewed by others and what to do to get that next promotion. (Agwai, 2023).

- **EXPOSURE: 60%—Manage your exposure, so the right people will know you.** Who knows about you and what you do? Does your boss know what you do? Does their boss know you and what you do? Do others inside and outside your organization know anything about you? Visibility is important. Take advantage to lead and manage company events, programs, organize social events, or write blogs in company newsletters. It is also important to be visible externally. Join a professional organization, run for office, or manage an event. The key is to be visible to the right people, in the right manner, at the right time. (Agwai, 2023).

Over the years, I've added another "P" to Performance, which is Proximity. Early in your career, and especially today, you must be close enough to observe what right looks like. Nehemiah was in proximity to the king, which is how he gained authority and approval to go rebuild the walls of Jerusalem. Timothy was in proximity to the Apostle Paul during his journey of salvation, which is how he became a giant in the body of Christ through the Apostle Paul's tutelage.

Jesus' Leadership Example

JESUS ACTED AS a Leader with a difference; he had a vision, mission, objectives, and strategies with a distinct and definite leadership style. Jesus' leadership style was characterized by compassion, love, and servanthood. This was Kingdom Leadership at its very best. The greatest leader this world has ever known, Jesus. In His short time on earth, He exhibited powerful traits. He exemplified integrity, honesty, generosity, purpose-giving, humility, inspiration, compassion, forgiveness, and so much more. This is a great contrast to what we would think of when we consider managers, leaders, and executives whom we have known or admired.

Kingdom Leadership is—
- Not about power but empowerment
- Not about control but service (servanthood)
- Not about titles but towels (JOHN 13:2-17)
- Not about pomp but people
- Not about manipulation but inspiration
- Not about position but purpose

Consider whom you would want to be compared to—a great world leader whose name has lived on for hundreds of years or the

King of all kings who continues a legacy unmatched? Of course, we choose Christ, but do our career choices reflect that?

Established about two thousand years ago, the movement initiated by Jesus Christ now has emerged into an illustrious and unrivaled organization named Christianity for the benefit of mankind, which steers the world with the Christian way of living. The style of leadership evolved and practiced by Jesus has strongly influenced every form of the organization, be it big or small, service, business, or family all through the past twenty centuries. It has universal significance and applicability based on strong foundations that stood the test of time and can be justified empirically. We are to live, love, and lead like Jesus, but what does that mean practically? One core truth that we must adhere to is that our success is not measured by worldly standards but by God and His Kingdom. Another trait is our obedience to God rather than to the world, other leaders, or even ourselves.

Multiple times in **PROVERBS (14:12, 16:25),** we are warned, "There is a way that seems right to a man, but its end is the way of death." It's not wise to trust anything above God and His ways. Each leader and/or employee is different. Jesus demonstrated it. Some of the disciples or staff got the message and some didn't. As Jesus demonstrated, you sometimes have to bring subordinates in and do a one-on-one session or desk-side brief. Jesus had to give Thomas a desk-side brief in order for him to believe the vision.

JOHN 20:24 *Now Thomas (also known as Didymus), one of the Twelve, was not with the disciples when Jesus came.* 25 *So the other disciples told him, "We have seen the Lord!" But he said to them, "Unless I see the nail marks in his hands and put my finger where the nails were, and put my hand into his side, I will not believe." 26 A week later his disciples were in the house again, and Thomas was with them. Though the doors were locked, Jesus came and stood among them and said, "Peace be with you!" 27 Then he said to Thomas, "Put your finger here; see my hands. Reach out your hand and put it into my side. Stop doubting and believe." 28 Thomas said to him, "My Lord and my God!" 29 Then Jesus told him, "Because you have seen me, you have believed; blessed are those who have not seen and yet have believed."*

As the Manager and CEO, sometimes you have to clean up what your staff messes up. Jesus had to fix what Peter messed up.

LUKE 22:50 *And one of them (Peter) smote the servant of the high priest, and cut off his right ear.* LUKE 22:51 *And Jesus answered and said, Suffer ye thus far. And he touched his ear, and healed him.*

Some leaders you will have to allow to go through the trial as Jesus permitted Peter, but He prayed for him. This was the greatest lesson in Peter's life.

LUKE 22:54 *Then they seized him and led him away, bringing him into the high priest's house, and Peter was following at a distance. 55 And when they had kindled a fire in the middle of the courtyard and sat down together, Peter sat down among them. 56 Then a servant girl, seeing him as he sat in the light and looking closely at him, said, "This man also was with him." 57 But he denied it, saying, "Woman, I do not know him." 58 And a little later someone else saw him and said, "You also are one of them." But Peter said, "Man, I am not." 59 And after an interval of about an hour still another insisted, saying, "Certainly this man also was with him, for he too is a Galilean." 60 But Peter said, "Man, I do not know what you are talking about." And immediately, while he was still speaking, the rooster crowed. 61 And the Lord turned and looked at Peter. And Peter remembered the saying of the Lord, how he had said to him, "Before the rooster crows today, you will deny me three times." 62 And he went out and wept bitterly. ESV*

This was one of the greatest lessons in Peter's life, and it produced the greatest change in his life. Jesus let him go. Sometimes letting people go is the best thing you can do for them and/or the organization. Letting someone go is one of the hardest things that you'll ever have to do as a manager. Handle the situation well and you'll minimize the uncertainty and disruption that it may cause for your team and your business. Contrariwise, manage it poorly, and the person you're letting go might feel shocked, confused, and belligerent. The person's self-esteem may be damaged, and revenge or retaliation against you or your organization may occur. Your professional reputation could be affected, and you may even lose the respect and loyalty of your team because you didn't handle the termination or dismissal appropriately.

No matter why someone is being dismissed, who made the decision, or how you feel about it personally, terminating the employment will likely fall to you as the manager. This is not a task that you can delegate! The person needs to hear the news from you directly and be given the chance to ask questions and air their thoughts and feelings. Jesus had to let Peter go, and as a result, Peter came back stronger. He also let Judas go, but he didn't make it back. Everyone will not respond the same, even under similar conditions.

> JOHN 13:21 *After saying these things, Jesus was troubled in his spirit, and testified, "Truly, truly, I say to you, one of you will betray me." 22 The disciples looked at one another, uncertain of whom he spoke. 23 One of his disciples, whom Jesus loved, was reclining at table at Jesus' side, 24 so Simon Peter motioned to him to ask Jesus of whom he was speaking. 25 So that disciple, leaning back against Jesus, said to him, "Lord, who is it?" 26 Jesus answered, "It is he to whom I will give this morsel of bread when I have dipped it." So when he had dipped the morsel, he gave it to Judas, the son of Simon Iscariot. 27 Then after he had taken the morsel, Satan entered into him. Jesus said to him, "What you are going to do, do quickly." 28 Now no one at the table knew why he said this to him. 29 Some thought that, because Judas had the moneybag, Jesus was telling him, "Buy what we need for the feast," or that he should give something to the poor. 30 So, after receiving the morsel of bread, he immediately went out. And it was night.*

When Peter came back, Jesus interviewed him for the job again. Since Peter had denied him three times, Jesus, the CEO and the

Son of God, presented to him three interview questions to ensure Peter had grown through his recent experience as a leader before rehiring him. Here are the interview questions:

1. Simon Peter, Simon, son of John, do you love me more than these?
2. Simon, son of John, do you love me?
3. Simon, son of John, do you love me?

Here is the interview with Peter's responses:

JOHN 21:15 *When they had finished breakfast, Jesus said to Simon Peter, "Simon, son of John, do you love me more than these?" He said to him, "Yes, Lord; you know that I love you." He said to him, "Feed my lambs." 16 He said to him a second time, "Simon, son of John, do you love me?" He said to him, "Yes, Lord; you know that I love you." He said to him, "Tend my sheep." 17 He said to him the third time, "Simon, son of John, do you love me?" Peter was grieved because he said to him the third time, "Do you love me?" and he said to him, "Lord, you know everything; you know that I love you." Jesus said to him, "Feed my sheep.*

Jesus made sure that he would be loyal to the company this time. This was the greatest lesson in Peter's life, and it produced the greatest change in his life. Often, your greatest wisdom will come out of your greatest failure.

Failure is not fatal, and failure is not final. Trouble can be a blessing in disguise. (PSALM 119:17)

Trials are intended:
- To reinforce our dependence upon God
- To awaken us up and make us think
- To wean us from the world
- To motivate us to read and study the Bible
- To drive us to our knees
- To produce humility in us
- To give us a fresh testimony of God's glory

Leadership Nucleus

LEADERSHIP NUCLEUS, ALSO known as the inner circle, is a small executive group of close friends or associates, normally two or three, close enough physically, spiritually, and emotionally to unburden yourself; this nucleus is a support to whom secrets are confided or with whom private matters are discussed.

Jesus had a nucleus: Peter, James, and John. He had twelve disciples on his staff, or executive board, but out of those twelve, he had three of them who were his nucleus. There are always a handful of confidants on your staff or team whom you will take with you where others cannot go. These are those whom you trust beyond the office. Your nucleus will be those in which you share your deepest thoughts, what bothers you, and things that may be highly confidential. Many times when Jesus took on things that required great faith, He brought in Peter, James, and John.

Make sure it's someone with honesty and integrity, whom you are 100% sure will be confidential about what you are sharing. Loose lips sink ships.

It is someone whom you can rely on, share with, lean into for tough decisions, gripe about things, and receive counsel from. Your nucleus is more prone to listening than talking. Advice and counsel many times can be best given by being a sounding board rather than a clanging gong.

There is an epidemic of loneliness among leaders, and the forces that fuel it are insidious. Executives spend their careers climbing ladders of success. They achieve results and recognition through hard work, grit, and collaboration. Nonetheless, when they reach the top of the ladder, they realize, ironically, they are more alone than ever. Unable to confide in board members or senior executives for fear of losing trust and hesitant to alert others to sensitive challenges, leaders often work through problems in a vacuum. Even the most inclusive leader can feel isolated and stuck.

Identify people inside and outside your organization in whom you can honestly and confidentially confide. These individuals become thought partners and sources of out-of-the-box solutions. They are agenda-less sounding boards to help refine ideas and identify landmines or unforeseen consequences. Here's where you can start your search:

1. Confide in those who believe in you but will challenge you and identify paths you have not explored.
2. Reach out to peers with similar roles outside your immediate field.
3. As you interact, don't just ask for advice, but offer your engagement.
4. Open up to trusted comrades and friends for recommendations.
5. Engage trusted friends who may know people outside your network who could be strong informal advisors.

Using the Wolf

WHILE INITIAL SIGNS and symptoms of rogue employees, also known as wolves in some cases, often go unnoticed or ignored by companies or organizations, it is vitally essential for leaders to identify them and take steps to prevent possible damage to their company or organization. Highly talented or ambitious employees who are not held accountable for actions and behaviors that support and reflect professionally on the organization, will eventually lose respect for the boss, consequently, choosing instead to undermine the direction, call their own shots, and manipulate others to follow their lead—forming a wolf pack. Not all highly valued employees are susceptible to this phenomenon. It's usually the ones with self-serving intentions.

Employees who are aware of their responsibility for the progress of the company or organization can do wonders when working together for its betterment. If an employee goes rogue and causes damage to the company, it can ruin the company's reputation and prevent other employees from enjoying the benefits of their hard work.

WHY YOU NEED TO HANDLE WOLVES. If wolves are not handled in a careful and timely manner, they can cause severe damage to the company or organization and its reputation. The following list displays the most common situations that wolves, also known here as rogue employees, create:

- Stealing and sharing confidential details with rivals
- Starting a social media campaign to defame the company or organization
- Causing division within the organization
- Embezzling money
- Destroying records of important documents
- Leaking information that traps the company in legal complications
- Stealing the company's clients
- Transferring the company's property in their name
- Working as a spy for a competitor or adversary

STEPS YOU SHOULD TAKE. Never ignore or underestimate the amount of destruction that can be caused by a wolf or rogue employee. Knowing how damaging it can be for you and your business, make sure to take the following steps to handle the situation in a wise manner:

1. **Bind Employees By Rules And Regulations**

   You need to realize that an efficient response is required by the company or organization if you have discovered fraud by an employee. Formulate rules and regulations that determine a code of conduct for employees, such as Non-Disclosure Agreements (NDA). An NDA creates the legal framework to protect ideas and information from being stolen or shared with competitors or third parties. The NDA agreement triggers a host of legal ramifications, including lawsuits, financial penalties, and even criminal charges which will deter most wolves. Make sure the rules and policies encompass all possible consequences of a breach before any employee succeeds at damaging the company.

2. **Be Vigilant**

   You must be most vigilant when it comes to protecting your business. Give the wolves something to do to exert their energy and keep them close and in view. Learn how to keep an eye on your employees without giving them hints about your suspicions. Make a committee for this particular assignment and train your managers to look out for symptoms among employees that can be alarming. Develop an effective vigilance system in the organization to monitor and prevent any possible money embezzlement. Run an internal audit whenever suitable for your business to have a clearer picture of where capital is being used and by whom.

3. **Prevention**

   If you can prevent the cause of the rogue behavior of any employee, you may also succeed at stopping the wolf from damaging your team. Train your human resources department to spot and anticipate issues that your employees might have. The ability of the human resources (HR) department to handle all the grievances of workers can become your biggest asset in fighting the possibility of rogue employees. Also, encourage your employees to share their problems with the company's counselor and HR office only, so that the disputes can be sorted out within the office. Once the disputes are settled within the office, nobody from outside will be able to tarnish your team, organization, or company.

4. **Formulate Policies For the Use Of Social Media**

   As an employer, it is your right to prevent any wolves from bringing unneeded attention to your company or business.

In the current age where social media is used excessively and for many purposes, it has become essential for companies to formulate policies regarding the use of social media by employees. Trends and platforms of social media keep changing, and employers should refresh their policies accordingly. Wolves may create bigger problems than an employer can handle, but it is always advisable to take suitable steps to prevent disputes and minimize potential damage through strict policies.

5. **Beware of Lone Wolves**

One of the challenges for new managers and one that is often not practically covered in leadership development programs is how to deal with a lone wolf on your team.

The Definition of a Lone Wolf. A lone wolf is an employee who contributes only marginally to the team's goals and accountabilities. Lone wolves are not team players. They focus on their own work, neglect team responsibilities, do not collaborate well with colleagues, rarely contribute to help others at team meetings, and do not join the effort when the team is under a deadline and needs extra help.

The Problem with Lone Wolves. Whatever negative behavior a non-team player is guilty of, you can't allow it to continue if being a team player is an essential part of your culture and strategy for success. Why? Because it's catching… You may well discover that the employee is poorly assigned and that he or she (and the team) would be better served in a different role. When you understand employees' skill sets, what they like to do, and where they could enthusiastically contribute, you can begin to explore better opportunities.

THE BOTTOM LINE New managers must avoid conflict with individuals who are not team players, wolves in sheep's clothing. Moreover, beware and don't let them set you up for failure. Take the steps now to address the situation. You and your team will be all the better for it.

Unwritten Rules

THERE ARE UNWRITTEN rules in leadership that are highly regarded, but not spoken openly or publicly during hiring or decision-making. First impressions and lasting impressions can be affected by the unwritten rules.

DRESS FOR SUCCESS. There are three basic colors for executive suits: Black, Navy, and Gray; all of which are versatile in mixing and matching color combinations, and each comes with its individual look and its own brand of psychological interpretation. Sometimes shades of brown or forest green will suffice. However, black is traditionally the color of authority and power.

Sticking with dark-colored suits, like black, navy, or charcoal gray for a formal event is recommended. For a day at the office, an all-black men's suit is too formal. Instead, I recommend wearing a gray or navy blue men's suit to work. Women can get away with far more colors in executive settings than men.

You will find that what you wear affects how you are received and perceived in meetings and events. Avoid bright vibrant colors and fancy hand-sewn designs, as they are best reserved for more formal occasions and not the workplace environment. Just like the rule for clothing colors, you must follow the same for ties and scarves. Flashy and bold colors don't look well on business suits.

BUSINESS CASUAL. The pants should complement the jacket, muted contrasting colors would work best, e.g. dark green jacket/gray trousers; Brown jacket/dark blue trousers. A general rule of thumb for business casual is to avoid loud and bright colors, such as yellow or red.

LEARN TO SAY, "I DON'T KNOW." Many young managers have not learned that they are not expected to know everything, but they should know where to point to give direction where one can start. It is okay to say, "I don't know" and take a "due out." That's Leadership 101. It is easier and safer to say, "I don't know, but I will find out," and take it as a due out. When you pretend to know and end up being strong and wrong, you lose credibility. Competence doesn't mean that you know everything; it simply means that you can be counted on to follow up and get the information needed. You will get better in time.

The bridge between a dream and reality is called action.
The bridge between knowledge and skill is called practice.
The bridge between skill and mastery is called time.

Don't be known as a good starter but a poor finisher. Constantly review developments to make sure that the actual benefits are what they are supposed to be. However menial and trivial your early assignments may appear, give them your best efforts. Be consistent on the level where you are and innovate. Operate within your ability, continue to develop your leadership skills, and stay current on modernization efforts. Persistence or tenacity is the disposition to persevere in spite of difficulties, discouragement, or indifference. In executing your project, don't wait for others; go after them, and make sure it gets done. Confirm the instructions that you give others, and their commitments, in writing. Don't assume it will get done!

BRIEFING TECHNIQUES. Stand with proper posture and respectfully take charge of the room. If you are sitting and you are the briefer, ensure that your seat is level with the listeners or slightly above to establish a command position psychologically as the briefer. Don't be timid; speak up. The fears that you don't face become your limits. Fear is nothing more than an invitation to evolve, grow, and broaden your horizon beyond what you have already mastered. Express yourself, and promote your ideas but respectfully. Often, those who confidently speak with knowledge will end up with the assignment. Strive for brevity and clarity in oral and written reports. Be extremely careful of the accuracy of your statements. Cultivate the habit of codifying matters down to the simplest terms. An elevator speech is the best way.

KEEP THE BOSS INFORMED. Don't overlook the fact that you are working for a boss. Keep him or her informed. Whatever the boss wants, within the bounds of integrity, takes top priority. Promises, schedules, and estimates are important instruments in a well-ordered business. Always spend time first exploring how it can be done, not how it can't. Don't bring a complaint without a suggestion standing beside it. Don't lean on the often-used phrase, "I can't estimate it because it depends upon many uncertain factors." Don't waste effort putting the finishing touches on something that has little substance to begin with. You can't polish a sneaker.

EMAILS AND MESSAGE ETIQUETTE. Never direct a complaint to the top. A serious offense is to "courtesy copy (cc)" a person's boss on a copy of a complaint before the person has a chance to respond to the complaint. You can burn valuable bridges this way that you might need to cross over during your career. When corresponding and dealing with outsiders, remember that you represent the company or organization. Be especially careful of your commitments. Because you represent the company, you can unknowingly obligate the company for something that cannot be legally fulfilled.

SOCIAL MEDIA: KEEP IT CLEAN. Your qualifications and experience should take center stage. Keep in mind that your character and representation of yourself play a huge role too. Your social media could be a look into your personality before employers have even met you. If you come across as negative, recruiters may question your interpersonal skills. Do employers check an applicant's social media posts? Yes, a high percentage of employers check an applicant's social media. Whether negative or positive, your social media presence could give employers a sense of your character. Although it's not the deciding factor in the hiring process, it could influence their decision. From inappropriate pictures to presumptuous posts, there are a number of ways that social media can damage your career or even hinder it from starting. Social media has become an important tool for recruitment agencies in recent years, but it has also created problems for irresponsible job seekers. We get it, your online accounts are for your personal use. For many, it's a place to joke around, but if that's who you really are, are you the perfect candidate? If you display a negative image, your social media can affect your job opportunities.

These include:

- **Inappropriate Photos:** Inappropriate social media photos reflect your character. Even if someone tags you with inappropriate photos online, it could paint a different picture of who you really are. Don't allow everyone to tag you with their posts on social media. Being professional in and outside of the workplace could work in your favor.
- **Rude Remarks and Posts:** If you love to stir the pot, you're in for some bad news. Employers seek candidates who are respectful and able to work well with others. Rude posts could make you seem irresponsible and unprofessional.

GRAMMAR AND SPELLING MISTAKES. Take advantage of writing classes offered in your organization, or invest in an executive writing class. Non-verbal communication is important in every workplace, whether you are writing reports or sending a professional email. Poor spelling and grammar could show that you aren't able to communicate effectively and clearly. Check your grammar, and use a spellcheck feature.

DECISION MAKING. Don't get excited when dealing with emergencies. Keep your feet on the ground. Get the facts and cultivate the habit of making quick, clean-cut decisions. When making decisions, the "pros" are much easier to deal with than the "cons." Your boss wants to see them both. When faced with decisions, try to look at them as if you were one level up in the organization. Imagine yourself on the other side of the table. Your perspective will change quickly.

EXERCISE YOUR THINKING—Use any two of these to get the third:
- Knowledge
- Time
- Money

SENSE OF HUMOR. Don't ever lose your sense of humor. Have fun at what you do. It will reflect in your work. Laugh a little. Like driving in the rain, the wipers don't stop the rain, but they make it where it doesn't stop you. That's what laughter does to the human soul. Don't be so focused on maximizing your days that it makes you mean and impatient with people; don't lose your humor. You remember ⅓ of what you read, ½ of what people tell you, but 100% of what you feel. No one likes a grump except another grump. Learn to smile. The formula for success is not about how much money you make; it's how you enjoy life and the lives you positively impact. A key to good management is to turn problems into opportunities.

> **❝** *The happiest people don't have the best of everything, they make the best of everything.*
> TONY ROBBINS

The Importance of Exercise for Leaders

DURING MY YEARS of working in the Pentagon, one of the most memorable moments of my tenure was when I first arrived, and the Vice Chief of Staff of the Army gave us our introductory brief. He stated, "Working in the Pentagon can be a stressful place; therefore, I am authorizing you three hours a week to exercise in the Pentagon Athletic Center." I later took him up on the offer and found that to be very true. During my tenure, exercise proved to be a good stress reliever and a very wise use of time. Leadership is a role often accompanied by stress and pressure. However, I have found that a physically fit leader is better equipped to manage stress effectively. Regular exercise has been proven to be an effective stress management tool, helping to reduce stress levels and improve overall well-being. When leaders engage in physical activity, they enhance their ability to handle the pressures of leadership, decreasing the likelihood of burnout and stress-related issues. By managing personal stress, leaders create an environment where their staff and team members can thrive and flourish. Various studies have explored the link between exercise and leadership performance. Results indicate that regular exercise can improve concentration and focus, reduce stress, and increase self-esteem. All of these attributes are essential to being an effective leader.

STRESS REDUCTION. Exercise is known to reduce stress, which can be especially important for leaders who often face high-pressure situations. Reduced stress levels can lead to improved decision-making and interpersonal skills. It also offers both short-term and long-term benefits for mental well-being. Engaging in regular exercise stimulates the release of endorphins, which naturally affect your mood, helping to reduce stress levels and promote a sense of calmness. Exercise also provides a healthy outlet for preventing mishaps, channeling negative emotions, and serves as a suppressant from everyday stressors. Additionally, physical activity improves sleep quality and helps regulate the body's stress response system by lowering cortisol levels. Over time, these combined effects contribute to a more temperance and balanced state of mind, allowing individuals to better cope with stress and maintain optimal mental health. For leaders and subordinates alike, incorporating physical activity into daily routines can significantly enhance their ability to manage stress, ultimately leading to improved decision-making and interpersonal skills.

RESILIENCE. Resilience is critical in today's leadership. Resilience is the ability of a person to adjust to or recover readily from illness, adversity, and major life changes. It is an essential quality for effective leadership, as it enables leaders to bounce back from setbacks and challenges. Physical fitness plays a significant role in building resilience. Exercise not only improves physical health but also enhances mental and emotional well-being. A physically fit leader is better equipped to overcome obstacles, persevere in the face of adversity, and inspire their staff and team members to do the same. By cultivating resilience through physical fitness, leaders foster a culture of perseverance and growth within their organizations.

CREATIVITY AND IMAGINATION. A study by the *Center for Creative Leadership* found that "leaders who exercise regularly were rated significantly higher by their bosses, peers, and direct reports on their leadership effectiveness than those who don't" (Leading Effectively Staff, 2020). This is key today for individuals in managerial roles to think more innovatively and develop creative solutions for complex issues, which is often required from successful business leaders in this era of modernization. Furthermore, physical activity contributes to improved decision-making skills and increased self-awareness by providing a platform for introspection and reflection on oneself. This enhances self-awareness and assists leaders to identify their strengths and weaknesses and effectively delegate tasks to others. As a result, they can better lead their subordinates and make informed decisions that benefit the organization or company.

BEING DISCIPLINED AND ORGANIZED. Personal exercise often involves setting goals, maintaining a routine, and developing self-discipline. These skills can be transferable to leadership roles, helping leaders stay organized and focused on their objectives. It is consistent with the commitment to routines and objectives. By engaging in regular exercise, individuals learn the importance of setting achievable goals and strategies, breaking them down into smaller steps, and persistently working towards their targets. This process not only helps improve physical fitness but also cultivates mental fortitude and self-discipline, as individuals overcome challenges and maintain motivation despite setbacks. Furthermore, the satisfaction derived from accomplishing fitness goals can bolster self-confidence and encourage the pursuit of other objectives in various aspects of life. The discipline and goal-oriented mindset developed through physical activity can be invaluable in leadership roles, as these skills are transferable to managing teams, setting organizational targets, and navigating complex challenges in the professional environment.

Leadership Practical Ideas to Help You Save Time and Energy:
* 3D Management Principle: Do It, Dump It, or Delegate It.
* Exercise Your Body and Mind at the Same Time.
* Use Commute Time as Learning Time.
* Give Your Body the Rest it Needs.
* Use a Task Manager to Keep Your Brain Clear.
* Get a Mentor or Coach.
* Dedicate a Distraction-free Zone in Your Home/Office.

SELF CONFIDENCE AND SELF ESTEEM. Personal exercise can boost self-confidence and self-esteem, both of which are important qualities for leaders to have. A confident leader is more likely to inspire trust and respect from their team. As individuals experience personal growth and development through the consistent pursuit of fitness goals, a confidence boost is usually achieved. Engaging in regular exercise not only improves physical strength and appearance but also instills a sense of accomplishment and self-efficacy. As individuals witness their progress and overcome obstacles in their fitness journey, they gain confidence in their abilities to tackle challenges and adapt to new situations. This heightened sense of self-assurance extends beyond the realm of physical fitness, positively influencing various aspects of life, including professional and social interactions. Confident individuals are more likely to take calculated risks, assert themselves effectively, and inspire trust in others. In the context of leadership, the confidence fostered through physical activity can contribute to effective decision-making, strong interpersonal relationships, and a commanding presence that motivates and galvanizes team members to achieve their collective goals.

TEAM BUILDING. Engaging in group exercises or sports can help leaders build strong relationships with their team members, fostering collaboration and teamwork. Engaging in shared physical activities creates opportunities for individuals to work together towards common goals, fostering collaboration, trust, and camaraderie among team members. Through these experiences, participants develop a better understanding of each other's strengths and weaknesses, allowing them to effectively support one another and adapt to various roles within the team. Moreover, group physical activities can also provide a platform for healthy competition, which can motivate individuals to push their limits and strive for excellence. Participating in team-based physical activities can help break down barriers and improve communication among team members, leading to a more cohesive and harmonious working environment. For leaders, taking part in these activities alongside their team members can strengthen interpersonal relationships, bridge hierarchical gaps, and demonstrate a commitment to the overall well-being and success of the team.

Note: When you are young, you spend your youth trying to get wealth; when you are old, you spend your wealth trying to regain health.

Brian Tracy teaches the five Ps of excellent health:
- Proper exercise
- Proper diet
- Proper weight
- Proper rest
- Proper attitude (Gray, 2011).

Resilience and Determination

RESILIENT AND DETERMINED leaders have the ability to sustain their energy level under pressure, cope with disruptive changes, and adapt. They don't spend time crying over spilled milk; they look for the next cow. They bounce back from setbacks and overcome major difficulties without engaging in dysfunctional behavior or harming others. At times, you will encounter individuals with rotten attitudes, but don't ever seek revenge on rotten people. Rotten fruit falls on its own. You don't have to throw rocks at it. It takes more strength to hold your tongue than to say every derogatory thing that you can think of. Remember, wisdom is knowing what to ignore.

Never use your background as an excuse not to succeed. Dare to succeed against the odds. We benchmark great leaders such as Abraham Lincoln, Dr. Martin Luther King Jr., and Nelson Mandela, among many others, who have proven the power of true resilience in the face of extreme adversity. These leaders did not just survive and adapt but also imprinted the true meaning of resilience in all walks of life. How you deal with adversity determines whether you grow, sail, or sink. Don't miscalculate your situation. If you get in trouble, become a student. Don't ask, "How did I get into this," ask, "What can I learn from this?" You don't have to see the whole staircase, just the next step. You must be determined to succeed.

During the early 1900's, a Native American, by the name of Jim Thorpe, endured extreme adversity (Dughi, 2016). By the age of 9, Jim's twin brother had died. Furthermore, both of his parents passed away a few years after his brother's death. Young Jim Thorpe became an orphan. To exacerbate these tragic occurrences, Jim suffered racial prejudice due to the color of his skin. Despite all of the hardships that he endured, he started running and eventually qualified to run in the track and field event for the 1912 Olympics.

It was the big day of the 1912 Olympic race. As Jim had set out that morning, striving to win the race ahead of him, he realized that his running shoes had been stolen. With not much time, he quickly looked for a resolution to this problem. He resulted in finding two shoes of different sizes in a trash can. Once again, he thought of another way to mitigate this new problem; he resorted to wearing an extra sock to caveat the extra space in the larger shoe. Despite this set of limitations, Jim put on both shoes, ran the race, and ended up winning two gold medals for the United States at the end of the day (Dughi, 2016).

The real success of your life will always be based on what you have left. In a plane, if the pilot loses an engine, he focuses on the one he has left to land the plane, not the one he lost.

❝ *Courage is not having the strength to go on; it's going on when you don't have the strength.*
THEODORE ROOSEVELT

Leadership from the Heart

THERE IS A need for leaders to connect with their teams from a place of heart, unity, and togetherness. Leading from the heart means leading from that place of engaging with your purpose, taking responsibility for your actions, taking care of those whom you lead, and learning how to trust your heartfelt instincts in times of trouble. A Kingdom Leader exemplifies unconditional love for the team and staff. This is what the Bible calls in the Greek "Agape" (unconditional love), which naturally has a positive effect on the team. Leaders who genuinely take a heartfelt interest in their employees and connect with them on an emotional level are leaders who not only will be remembered by their employees but will experience high performance from them. Leaders are likely to experience shifts in instinct where they make better decisions, think differently, are inclusive, and develop an innate ability to spot talent in the organization through heightened discernment.

When there is no feeling or emotion in an organization, the level of engagement and joy in that organization or business will be limited or nonexistent. The impact that the heart can have in an organization is phenomenal: It can not only accelerate efficiency, effectiveness, and corporate revenues but also engagement levels in the organization, impacting everyone from troops to employees to customers.

During my tenure in the Pentagon, at the close of the Afghanistan war for several months, the Department of Defense hosted the Wounded Warrior Day on Fridays. We would celebrate and honor soldiers in the halls of the Pentagon in Army Corridor three with cheers, applause, and many tears every Friday morning. At this instant, the entire length of the corridor is packed with leaders—officers, a few sergeants, and civilians, all crammed tightly, three and four deep against the walls. Everyone shifted to ensure an open path remained down the center.

The clapping started at the E-Ring in the Pentagon. That is the outermost of the five rings of the Pentagon, and it is closest to the entrance to the building. This was applause with deep emotion and sentiment behind it, as it moved forward in a wave down the length of the hallway.

As I listened and watched, a steady rolling wave of sound moved at the pace of the soldier in the wheelchair who marked the forward edge with his presence. He is the first in the line of wounded warriors. He is missing the greater part of one leg, and some of his wounds are still healing. Behind him and stretching the length from Rings E to A, come more of his peers; each private, corporal, or sergeant was assisted as needed by a family member or another soldier. I then noticed a wounded soldier coming through whose hand had been blown off in battle. He had a hook for a hand, smiling, and shaking everyone's hand with it. I met his gaze and nodded as I applauded. When he got to me and shook my hand, I was nearly overcome with emotion. Here I stood with the use of all my limbs, but this young man who was missing a limb, still found something to smile and rejoice about, life. This event changed my leadership passion from the heart and reiterated how important Kingdom Leadership is. As a leader who wrote policy for the Department of the Army, developed processes, and managed programs and people, I realized how critical it is that we get it right…that we care. If the well-being of the Soldier was not our passion, priority, and focus, we were in the wrong business. I've shared this moment in time at several events and conferences that I have been honored to speak. If we as leaders don't have passion and get our policies, programs, and processes wrong, we could lose those who follow along after us. Thousands more would come home on stretchers, horribly wounded, and facing months or years in military hospitals.

No one in that hallway, walking or clapping, was ashamed by the silent tears on more than a few cheeks. Soldiers and Department of Defense Civilians wiped their eyes only to see better. A couple of the Soldiers in the crowd had themselves been a part of this parade in the past. We welcomed them home.

This parade went on several Fridays, for months, but gave us a reality of passion and the cost of true leadership.

Always stay true and consistent with principles that should never change.

Here are five key leadership life principles:
- Never lose your honesty
- Never lose your loyalty
- Never lose your compassion for people
- Never lose your humility
- Never lose your integrity

In **MATTHEW 20:25-28**, Jesus tells His disciples that leaders should not exercise authority over people. Instead, whoever wants to become great must humble himself to be a servant. Serving others is the only way to lead with a pure heart, free of pride and arrogance. That's Kingdom Leadership.

Final words from the CEO:

Commit your work to the Lord, and your plans will be established.
PROVERBS 16:3

But first and most importantly seek (aim at, strive after) His kingdom and His righteousness [His way of doing and being right—the attitude and character of God], and all these things will be given to you also. MATTHEW 6:33 (AMP)

Trust in the Lord with all your heart, and do not lean on your own understanding. In all your ways acknowledge him, and he will direct your paths. PROVERBS 3:5-6

Bibliographical Notes

Chapter 5: Potential: Use What Is in Your Hand

The Province, Vancouver, British Columbia (September 19, 1990),
https://www.newspapers.com/newspage/502569253/

Chapter 9: Humility in Leadership

APA Dictionary of Psychology. *American Psychological Association, American Psychological Association*, dictionary.apa.org/humility. Accessed 25 Aug. 2023.
Mayo, Margarita. "If Humble People Make the Best Leaders, Why Do We Fall for Charismatic Narcissists?" *Harvard Business Review*, 20 July 2017, hbr.org/2017/04/if-humble-people-make-the-best-leaders-why-do-we-fall-for-charismatic-narcissists.
Ou, Amy Y., et al. "Do humble CEOs matter? an examination of CEO humility and firm outcomes." *Journal of Management*, vol. 44, no. 3, 2018, pp. 1147–1173, https://doi.org/10.1177/0149206315604187.

Chapter 10: The Importance of People Skills

Sturt, David, and Todd Nordstrom. "10 Shocking Workplace Stats You Need to Know." *Forbes, Forbes Magazine*, 8 Mar. 2018, www.forbes.com/sites/davidsturt/2018/03/08/10-shocking-workplace-stats-you-need-to-know/?sh=4fbf0a49f3af.
Taylor, Shannon, et al. "Why People Get Away with Being Rude at Work." *Harvard Business Review*, 10 July 2019, hbr.org/2019/07/why-people-get-away-with-being-rude-at-work.

"What Type of Leader Are You?—Try Our Leadership Quiz—Oak Engage."
Oak Digital Workplace, Oak Engage, 28 Sept. 2022,
www.oak.com/blog/what-type-of-leader-are-you/.
Greenhouse, Emily. "The Neglected Suicide Epidemic." *The New Yorker*,
13 Mar. 2014,
www.newyorker.com/news/news-desk/the-neglected-suicide-epidemic.

Chapter 13: Fight in Your Weight Class
Rusth, Shanie. "Boxing Weight Classes Explained: Boxing 101." FightCamp,
FightCamp, 12 Oct. 2022, blog.joinfightcamp.com/fight-news/boxing-
weight-classes-explained-boxing-101/.

Chapter 18: PIE Theory
Agwai, Gladys. "Why Your Success Requires You Eat the Whole p.i.e."
Businessday NG, 13 Feb. 2023, businessday.ng/life-arts/article/why-your-
success-requires-you-eat-the-whole-p-i-e/.

Chapter 23: The Importance of Exercise for Leaders
Leading Effectively Staff. "A Leader's Best Bet: Exercise." CCL, 16 Nov. 2020,
www.ccl.org/articles/leading-effectively-articles/spotlight-on-exercise-and-
leadership/.
Gray, Nakkia. "The Five 'PS' to Stay Healthy, Happy and Motivated." From
the Masters, Beliefnet, Inc. and/or its licensors, 13 Oct. 2011,
www.beliefnet.com/columnists/fromthemasters/2011/10/the-five-ps-to-stay-
healthy-happy-and-motivated.html.

Chapter 24: Resilience and Determination
Dughi, Paul. "Olympics Flashback: Jim Thorpe Won Two Gold Medals with
Shoes Someone Had Thrown in the Trash." Medium, SportsRaid, 7 June
2016, medium.com/sportsraid/when-jim-thorpe-won-two-gold-medals-with-
shoes-someone-had-thrown-in-the-trash-3c3f7090f9e7.